THE

# Z E N

OF

# PROPOSAL
# WRITING

# THE ZEN OF

# PROPOSAL WRITING

An Expert's Stress-Free Path

to Winning Proposals

With a Special Section

on Presenting Your

Ideas in Person

## KITTA REEDS

 THREE RIVERS PRESS • NEW YORK

Published by Three Rivers Press, New York, New York.
Member of the Crown Publishing Group, a division of Random House, Inc.
www.randomhouse.com

THREE RIVERS PRESS and the Tugboat design are registered trademarks of Random House, Inc.

Printed in the United States of America

*Design by Barbara Sturman*

Library of Congress Cataloging-in-Publication Data
Reeds, Kitta.
   The Zen of proposal writing : an expert's stress-free path to winning : with a special section on presenting your ideas in person / by Kitta Reeds.
Includes bibliographical references.
1. Proposal writing for grants.     I. Title.
   HG177.R44     2002
   658.15'224—dc21

2002002306

ISBN  0-609-80649-1

10  9  8  7  6  5  4  3  2  1

First Edition

For Kevin and Jenna and Maia

And for Rob Schmidt, who really

*was* a rocket scientist

*The Tao, without doing anything,*
*Leaves nothing undone.*
—Lao-tzu

*Whatever you can do, or think you can do—begin it.*
*For boldness has power and magic and genius in it.*
—Goethe

# Acknowledgments

Many people helped me write this book. I owe them my thanks and much more. Lavish lunches and trips to faraway beaches have been suggested.

My thanks to Sam Fleishman, an agent who encouraged me to expand a short article into this book. I owe gratitude to the people who read the book proposal or the first drafts of the book: Barbara Hansen, Maia Mandoli, Marlys Mayfield, Chris Peterson, Jenna Reeds, Kevin Reeds, and Diane Young. They pulled it out of me and kept me going. Elise Hansen was heroic in plowing through the manuscript several times, always finding something I missed. Michael Smith made sensitive changes that saved me from making a perfect fool of myself. The remaining mistakes are all mine.

My thanks to Tad Windes for much help with deadlines over the years (all those folders and FedEx packages); to Fran Magee for listening with wisdom; and to all the researchers, editors, typists, and proofreaders who taught me to be an editor. My appreciation to the Maui Writers Conference for inspiration and tangible help. I thank Kathryn Henderson, editor at Three Rivers Press, for making me work harder to make the book stronger, and Linda Mead for being a superb agent.

Thanks to the Su Hong Reading Regulars: Jean, Jody, Linda, Mark, Ralph, and Rick, who supplied me with diverting thrillers, and Fred and David, who supplied the wine.

A special thanks to my longtime friend Gene Williams, who prodded me to keep sending out the book proposal to anyone and everyone. He told me to hang around bus stations: "Hey, mister, wanna see a book proposal?"

# Contents

# Foreword

This book gives you a new, relaxed approach to writing a proposal or preparing a presentation. In a playful way, this book conveys the spirit of Zen as described best by Jon Winokur in *Zen to Go*:

> Zen is simple and unpretentious. It's friendly. It doesn't take itself too seriously. It doesn't sit on its behind in some shrine, it gets in and mingles. It's flexible and portable, but it isn't junk food for the soul, it's hearty spiritual nourishment. It has dignity, a sense of humor, and a gritty iconoclastic spirit.

You'll learn a sort of nonaction, seemingly purposeless approach—a stress-free way to have fun by going through simple steps that require no commitment. Before you realize it, you'll have that proposal or presentation done and it's showtime!

If you thrive on multitasking, you can skip around in this book, sampling chapters as you please. Each chapter applies one Zen concept to one facet of proposal preparation, illustrated by excerpts from proposals that won and proposals that lost, interviews with successful proposal writers, and advice from people who have the power to accept or reject proposals.

This book is lighthearted—just as Zen is—because I believe you'll remember more if it makes you laugh. But because you are a busy, goal-directed person, you'll also find practical advice and solid examples in keeping with the down-to-earth practicality of Zen.

The stories and examples in this book come from my experience as a technical editor and technical writer for scientists, engineers, business consultants, and book authors. The stories are true and the examples are real, although I've sometimes changed a few nouns to disguise the writer. I've also drawn on what I learned as a trainer—teaching English to Japanese high school girls, teaching writing to American firefighters, and being a writing consultant to Japanese marketing representatives in Japan. I've included revelations from people who have attended my "Writing Winning Proposals" workshops.

Many other books tell you how to write proposals. This book shows you how to write winning proposals while staying serene. You will learn to laugh out loud at schedule disasters. You will learn how to write a proposal or give a talk without falling apart, without deserting your family, and without losing your Zen cool.

# PREPARE
# THE MIND

Do the Thinking That Makes

the Writing Do Itself

# First You Empty the Cup

## GETTING RID OF YOUR PRECONCEPTIONS ABOUT PREPARING PROPOSALS

*A professor who wanted to learn about Buddhism visited Nan-in, a famous Zen Master. When they were seated for tea, Nan-in began pouring tea into the professor's cup and kept on pouring even as the cup overflowed.*

*Finally, the professor said, "Don't you see the cup is overflowing?"*

*Nan-in said, "Like this cup, you are full of your own ideas about Buddhism. I cannot teach you anything until you first empty your cup."*

A proposal is anything you write to persuade someone to do what you want: publish your book, give you a grant, sign the contract, advance you the money, make bail for you, or let you keep the puppy. We all write proposals. Sometimes with a deadline, sometimes not. Sometimes under fear of rejection—no, always with fear of rejection. Sometimes with fear of acceptance: Can I really write this book? Can I actually do this project? And we all write under pressure. The good news is that pressure doesn't *have* to equal stress.

Over my twenty-five years of helping people sell their ideas, I've seen otherwise stable, highly intelligent people rage at colleagues or whimper in corners when they are working on a proposal. They leap at sudden noises, they cannot eat at all, or they eat pizza all night. The proposal becomes *all*. Yet through all this, they do write good proposals. They bring in contracts and grants, offers from book publishers, and venture capital. But does it need to be such an omigod-my-life-is-at-stake-here serious business?

When people take their writing too seriously, they often provoke unintended images like this racy idea, in a proposal to refine a new weapon for the military:

> The [weapon] could be effective at shorter ranges, but only if one makes the questionable assumption that the crews would be willing to expose themselves while attacking.

What writers in this state of tension need is some distancing from their writing. They need to center themselves, to sit quietly on a black cushion, and to breathe deeply and slowly. The serenity of Zen would allow them to see their sentences clearly *before* the proposal goes out to the potential buyer.

The Zen techniques presented in this book will allow you to produce your best work without the distractions of frenzy and tension. But to become open to acquiring these techniques, you first need to get rid of the old ideas that hold you back—what Zen calls "wrong thinking."

## WRONG THINKING

If you say you've never written a proposal, I'll bet you have. You've written a résumé and cover letter. That's a proposal. It's saying: "I want that job; here's why you should hire me." You probably wrote a letter from college asking Mom or Dad for just one more check to see you through the quarter. That's a proposal. I wrote my first proposal from summer camp when I was nine years old. It said: "I hate it here. Come take me home." They didn't, but I learned to write better proposals.

Because you're an old pro at proposals, I want you to forget most of what you've learned. Why? Because we all carry wrong thinking about writing proposals. We are convinced proposal writing must be stressful because (check all that apply):

> Trust yourself. You know more than you think you do.
>
> —Opening sentences of *Dr. Spock's Baby and Child Care*

❑ Writing proposals is scary and difficult. It makes sense to be afraid when we write.

❑ Writing a proposal is putting your soul on the line.

❑ The presentation must be perfect.
❑ We must write our very best stuff all the time.
❑ A proposal must be written at the last minute under extreme stress.
❑ Proposal writing is hell.

I won't pretend proposal writing is my preferred way to relax. You won't find it listed as one of the activities at Club Med. Imagine the full-color ad, showing an azure sea and a white beach filled with beautiful, tanned people, all holding laptops. The caption reads:

Treasure a leisurely afternoon in the sun, writing a Statement of Work. Relish an evening under the stars, revising your credentials section.

## FINDING EMPTINESS

Proposal writing isn't paradise, but it doesn't need to be hell, either. What I want you to forget about writing proposals is the old baggage that holds us back from working easily. Here's a Zen story.

> I always do the first line well, but I have trouble doing the others.
>
> —MOLIÈRE

Two monks were once traveling down a muddy road in heavy rain. At the joining of two roads, they met a lovely girl in a silk kimono, unable to cross the muddy intersection.

"Come on, girl," said the first monk. He lifted her in his arms and carried her over the mud.

The second monk did not speak again until late that night when they were back at the temple. Then he burst forth. "We monks should not go near females. It is dangerous. Why did you do that?"

"I left the girl there," said the first monk. "Are you still carrying her?"

I want you to forget so much about writing proposals that you achieve emptiness. In Zen, there is a lot of talk about emptiness and nothingness:

• The Zen saying *Shin ku myo u* means "From true emptiness, the wondrous being appears."

- Shunryu Suzuki wrote, "Moment after moment, everything comes from nothingness. This is the true joy of life."
- A Zen poem: If you have not / linked yourself / with true emptiness, / you will never understand / the Art of Peace.

We usually see emptiness as meaning depleted, lacking something important, lost, drained. But Zen emptiness means an open space, a zone of freedom, an area not cluttered.

We long for that kind of emptiness, but we seem afraid of it. We keep trying to cocoon over the weekend, to find that deserted beach. Then we take our laptops and cell phones with us.

Club Med advertises no radio, no television, no newspapers: "You can leave your watch at home!" But the Club Med I booked in the Bahamas scheduled tennis lessons at precisely nine o'clock each morning and scuba lessons at ten. La Boutique was open only from four to six in the afternoon and Le Banque from five to seven. To have lunch over at the boat dock, you had to sign up before six the night before.

Even on vacation, we have trouble accepting emptiness. How can you expect to do it when writing a proposal?

> How many times have you tried to shield yourself by reading the newspaper, watching television, or just spacing out? That is the $64,000 question: How much have you connected with yourself?
>
> —CHÖGYAM TRUNGPA

## REJECTING EMPTINESS

You don't have to, of course. You can choose to go on writing proposals in hell. Here are three ways:

- You can decide to suffer.
- You can insist on perfection.
- You can create frenzy.

### Deciding to Suffer

When I was little, my mother braided my hair every morning, then pinned the braids across the top of my head. It hurt. I was sure those bobby pins were piercing my skull and I complained forcefully. When my mother was in a hurry, she said, "Just hush." When she was relaxed, she smiled and said, "Remember, one must suffer to be beautiful." I could not imagine this was true unless you were a member of some tribe that glorified face carving.

In high school, I came upon the French saying *Il faut souffrir d'être belle.* Could my mother have been telling the truth? But no, the teacher said it really meant that one must have suffered to be truly beautiful. It had nothing to do with sticking bobby pins straight through your skull.

A beautiful proposal does not insist on your suffering. However, you can choose to suffer as you write, and most writers do. Fran Lebowitz says:

> All of life, as far as I'm concerned, is an excuse not to write. I just write when fear overtakes me. It causes paralytic terror. It's really scary just getting to the desk—we're talking now five hours. My mouth gets dry, my heart beats fast. I react psychologically the way other people react when the plane loses an engine.

In *It's Easier Than You Think: The Buddhist Way to Happiness*, Sylvia Boorstein paraphrases Buddha as saying, "Pain is inevitable, but suffering is optional."

Preparing a proposal demands focused energy and hard work, like chopping wood or carrying water. Suffering while writing a proposal wastes energy, but if it makes you feel noble, go for it.

## Insisting on Perfection

Striving to make your proposal perfect from the outset is guaranteed to cause suffering because you are bucking one of the natural laws of the universe—entropy. I first heard about entropy in a fine speech by Howard, an environmental chemist. He demonstrated entropy by opening a bottle of perfume and waving it in front of each of us. "Now," he said, "the molecules from the perfume are dissipating into the air. You can smell the perfume as the molecules enter your nose, but you cannot organize them back into the bottle. This is entropy. This is the natural disorder of the universe."

Wow. I loved the idea that it is natural for the universe to slowly run down to randomness and that disorder is natural law. I always thought I was just a sloppy person. But if disorder is natural, those fuzz balls under my bed are all part of a natural design. That disjointed paragraph, that muddy sentence—all part of a universal plan.

If you are writing a naturally disordered proposal, you are in tune with the universe. You can write serenely, knowing you will make it better when you start to refine it. If you insist on perfection, however, you will achieve perfect suffering.

## Creating Frenzy

Some proposal writers enjoy the adrenaline rush of proposal deadlines. They find that procrastination leads to excitement, and they like being the center of the whirlwind while everyone waits for them to finish their proposal.

There is another way. You can work in orderly panic, in a serene rush. You can work with what lawyers call "deliberate haste." But for the writers who crave frenzy, here are ways to guarantee it.

If you are writing a proposal alone, your opportunities for creating frenzy are limited but clear. Just put off writing the proposal. Agonize about it at three in the morning, but don't put any words on paper. Once you start writing, interrupt your writing to do more research. Spend most of your time on research so that you must finish the proposal in one all-night spurt just before it's due. Now you can send out a proposal that's not your best work, but you have a wonderful excuse: There was no more *time*. When you read the proposal a week later, you can enjoy great suffering while you notice all its faults.

Far more opportunities for creating frenzy are available when you write a proposal on a corporate team. Here are three of the best methods I've culled over the years. First, keep any of the client's specifications or the instructions given in the formal Request for Proposal (RFP) secret from your coauthors and all the people who must handle contractual or cost issues until the day the proposal is due out the door. Frenzy is guaranteed when they discover all the things they need to do very quickly so the proposal will meet the RFP requirements.

Second, give the editor an electronic early draft of

> I went for years not finishing anything. Because, of course, when you finish something, you can be judged.
>
> —ERICA JONG

your proposal, but continue rewriting your proposal *on-line*. A week later, give the editor your new version so he can guess where you made all those changes. A third version of the proposal, delivered late on the last day, will cause your editor to throw up his hands and "just let the damn thing go out as it stands."

Bronwyn, who was an editor for this type of proposal writer and is now a prosecuting attorney, said, "It's like trying to edit a river as it flows past you. You never enter the same proposal twice."

Third, don't read the RFP requirements, but take a sincere approach. Here are e-mail messages between Elizabeth, a technical editor, and Darcy, a proposal writer.

| | |
|---|---|
| Date: | January 4  4:02 P.M. |
| To: | Darcy |
| From: | Elizabeth |
| Re: | NASA Proposal |

Darcy, I've looked quickly through your proposal. It doesn't seem to follow the RFP requirements at all. Could I have the wrong RFP?

| | |
|---|---|
| Reply | < NASA Proposal January 4  4:58 P.M. |
| To: | Elizabeth |
| From: | Darcy |

Well, I tried following the outline in the RFP, but it just didn't seem LOGICAL to me. They want me to tell them the expected results before I've explained everything thoroughly. This is a complex concept, and I think I really need the Background section first so the reviewer will truly understand it all. Don't you think that makes sense?

| | |
|---|---|
| Reply | << NASA Proposal 5:14 P.M. |
| To: | Darcy |
| From: | Elizabeth |

I can certainly see your problem, but the RFP is very clear. They want the first section to give the objectives and the second section to describe the benefits to NASA's space mission. Our 37-page Background section will make the reviewer wait a LONG time to hear the benefits. How about we just move your Expected Results section on page 52 forward and rename it Benefits?

What concerns me MORE are the three sections that aren't even required by the RFP. Where do they come from?

Reply      <<< NASA Proposal 5:30 P.M.
To:      Elizabeth
From:      Darcy

To tell the truth, I actually structured this proposal to match the one I wrote to the EPA a while back.

Date:      January 4    6:02 P.M.
To:      Elizabeth
From:      Darcy
Re:      NASA Proposal

Elizabeth, did you get my last message? I haven't heard back from you.

Reply      <<<< NASA Proposal 6:30 P.M.
To:      Darcy
From:      Elizabeth

Sorry, Darcy. I just took a slow walk out in the fresh night air. While I was walking, I was wondering if perhaps you may have simply lost your mind.

     Your proposal to the EPA was written almost two years ago, to a different government agency, and on a different RFP. Why would you think responding to that old RFP would be a good idea NOW?

Reply      <<<<< NASA Proposal 6:35 P.M.
To:      Elizabeth
From:      Darcy

Because THAT proposal won!

Reply      <<<<<< NASA Proposal 6:37 P.M.
To:      Darcy
From:      Elizabeth

Hoo boy.

Here are two last-minute surefire techniques for creating frenzy.

One, *plan* for a last-second delivery. Allow no cushion of time for the unexpected earthquake or hurricane. Better yet, volunteer to hand-carry the proposal to the client yourself so that when your flight is diverted from Washington, D.C., to Philadelphia, you can be the hero who rents a four-wheel-drive and gets the proposal there through the blizzard.

Two, *plan* to be out of town at some important time during proposal preparation. The best choice is the last week before the proposal is due. That way, you'll be unavailable to answer questions or make any important decisions about the proposal. Next best is to schedule a presentation to a different client on another coast the next-to-last week before the proposal is due. This plan not only distracts you from the proposal during the crucial writing period so that you can work on your presentation, it also allows you to make glorious last-minute changes when you return from your trip. These changes should require the contracts people to rewrite the contract and the costing people to reestimate the cost. *Insist* on these changes. You can truthfully say, "But I was away when you made those decisions."

## SIMPLE WAYS TO MAKE YOUR PROPOSAL GO SMOOTHLY

You can continue to enjoy the surges of adrenaline as you race through producing a proposal in a whirlwind of frenzy. Or you can choose to empty the cup of all that wrong thinking about writing proposals in hell and try some simple new ideas. Like Zen itself, these ideas sound too simple to be effective—until you try them.

Start early. Like today. Most grant deadlines are the same year after year. Give yourself the whole year to write that proposal instead of squeezing it into the last month. Sometimes, of course, a client really needs a proposal yesterday. Reserve your rush proposals for those rare times. As an editor, I allowed each proposal writer three "miracles" a year. When they came to me with a rush-rush proposal, I asked them, "Are you sure you want this proposal to use up one of your three miracles?" Often, the deadline became negotiable.

Set a firm deadline even if your proposal doesn't have one. Make this a reasonable schedule and build in a special reserve of slack time for emergencies. When you do have an emergency (and you will), it will be simply interesting rather than disastrous.

Set lots of interim deadlines. Meeting each small deadline will give you the confidence to stay on schedule.

Plan to send the proposal at least two days before it's due. The guaranteed overnight courier services are remarkably good, and their record is 99 percent on-time delivery. But my company sends out about four hundred courier packages a week. A 1 percent error rate could mean four proposals don't make it on time. *But it's guaranteed!* Yes, and that means you get your $32.50 back, but you don't get another chance to bid on that million-dollar proposal.

If you must stay up all night to write your proposal, do it *early* in the schedule, not late, so you have time to fix all those mistakes you made at three in the morning.

Accept all the help you can get. Build in time for reviews by people who are not connected with writing the proposal. In companies that write proposals to the government, these people are called the Red Team. After the Blue Team writes the proposal, the Red Team reviews it, points out all the weaknesses, and sends the Blue Team back to write it over. Advice from the Red Team always makes me slap my hand to my forehead: "Of course, why didn't I see that?"

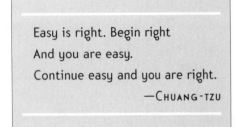

Easy is right. Begin right
And you are easy.
Continue easy and you are right.
—Chuang-tzu

If you're not on a corporate team and don't have a Red Team handy, create your own any way you can. Impose on your friends, other writers, co-workers, neighbors, your mail carrier—anyone who can see your proposal with a fresh eye.

## WHAT TO REMEMBER

Empty the cup to let go of your preconceptions about proposal writing. Writing a proposal does not need to be painful. To write serenely, you can change your outlook by making some simple choices:

- Decide to avoid suffering. Just work hard chopping wood and carrying water.
- Forget perfection. Even the most carefully prepared proposal will still have a few crumbs left in the butter. Clean it up as best you can, then let it go.
- *Plan* to forgo frenzy.

# Beginner's Mind

**2**

**WHERE I STARTED**

●

*If your mind is empty, it is always ready for something; it is open to everything. In the beginner's mind there are many possibilities, but in the expert's there are few.*

—SHUNRYU SUZUKI

●

In the last chapter, we learned to empty the cup—to empty our minds of the need to suffer while writing a proposal. Now we need to learn how to keep that cup empty by having a beginner's mind.

Here are the best ways I've learned to maintain a beginner's mind:

- Stay open to learning something new.
- Stay open to change.
- Accept. Let be.

Let me tell you some stories about how I learned to stay a beginner.

## STAY OPEN TO LEARNING SOMETHING NEW

I enter the proposal world with a beginner's mind by becoming a junior secretary for a nonprofit research institute. This world is all new to me. The bulletin board has requests for volunteers to taste fallout shelter food, sit in a smog chamber, or answer questions about dyeing their hair. I work with a group of molecular physicists in ancient military hospital buildings left over from World War II. Like Zen monks shaving each other's heads, the physicists take turns cutting each other's hair in one corner of the lab while they plan backpacking trips into the Sierras.

During my second week on the job, the monkeys escape from the life sciences building. They are all over the oak trees, chattering and swinging to higher and higher branches. We run outside to watch. Just as the animal rescue people prepare to shoot tranquilizer darts at the monkeys, an earth scientist starts a chant, "Don't shoot them! Don't shoot!" We all join in the chant. A biologist comes out with a bag of monkey food and lures them down from the trees. When the monkeys are all collected and everything settles down, we have more monkeys than we started out with.

So by my third week, I am only mildly surprised to walk into my boss's office and see three bearded men who appear to be playing paper dolls. One tears scribbled sheets from yellow legal pads and cuts them into strips. The second scatters the strips in piles about the table, and the third tapes them onto other yellow sheets. It seems they are writing a proposal, and this is the way they are organizing the list of references.

They write the proposal by hand on legal pads, and I type the words onto yellow draft paper. This draft is then overscribbled in ink by the proposal writers and attacked in red pencil by the editor. Long snaky lines move this sentence up and this paragraph down until no one can find their way. I retype it. Now they cut the paragraphs apart and paste them back in a different order.

I am not sure what this first proposal is about. The pages are filled with complex equations separated by passages that sound to me like something from *Alice in Wonderland:*

> Under brillig conditions, the toves are found to be slithy[1] and do, indeed, gyre.[2] However, they have been found[3-8] to gimble only if allowed to stand overnight in the wabe. We propose to examine mimsy borogoves (MBGs), so that we can contrast them with the outgrabe behavior of mome raths (OBMRs).

Work on the proposal builds to sixteen-hour days. The researchers kindly bring me Swiss chocolates and offer instant coffee mixed with lab alcohol. Once, the latest version of the proposal is lost for eight hours (no mega–copy machines or computer printouts then), but we find it in the trunk of the chemical physicist's car. Toward the end, I become so weary, I am convinced that sending copies numbered 1 through 5 to the client will give them only four copies. A woman with a doctorate in differential equations is brought over to reason with me.

Five days before the proposal is due, the researchers and I carry the proposal to the pressroom, where it is printed on a big offset press. We take the five copies over to the mailroom (FedEx is far in the future). As we walk away, the researchers are relaxed and joking. I realize only I have been frantic and frazzled. Although their jobs depend on winning this proposal, these guys have been having a wonderful time through the whole proposal process.

I wonder if I can learn to have fun under proposal pressure. Yes, I can. I begin to watch and to learn. I learn to stay open to learning something new.

## STAY OPEN TO CHANGE

Just as I thought I was becoming an expert on proposals, two things changed. I became a technical editor, and computers came along. I was a beginner again.

The operating system of our first word processor is four feet long and three feet high. People are afraid to walk near it. We decide to produce an important proposal on the new word processor, but we'll also have it typed by the typing pool, just to be safe. The word-processing team becomes secretive, keeping everyone else out of that room and speaking a new language of bits and bytes and escape keys.

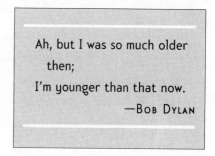

Ah, but I was so much older then;
I'm younger than that now.
—Bob Dylan

The typists are mostly older ladies. Thelma, the head of the typing pool, can spot a typo just by glancing over a typist's shoulder as she walks by. Maude has moved to the quiet world of the typing pool after twenty years of being a high-powered secretary. Gladys, already certified as the world's greatest typist, has five years to go before retiring. They vow to beat the word-processing machine before it can steal their jobs.

The word-processing team is ahead of the typing team for two days, until the machine suffers a setback over reformatting. The typists surge ahead, fingers flying. On the third day, the computer technicians solve the problem. The word-processing team now claims they'll have the proposal done in three hours. When the typists overhear the news, they take their first coffee break in two days. After a short prayer meeting, they decide it is their duty to keep on typing.

At four o'clock, the word-processing team announces they are ready to print the final copy. Gladys bursts into tears, her teardrops falling into her electric typewriter. The lights flicker and darken briefly; the typewriter shudders but resumes its purr.

Rumors come drifting up the hall. Typists gather in their doorway, trying to decipher the shouting from the end of the hall. Thelma sends them back to their typewriters and creeps up the hall to listen.

"What do you mean it won't print?"

"I didn't say it won't print, you idiot. I just said I can't find it. Anywhere!"

"Oh Jesus, let me try."

Thelma tiptoes back to the others: "They've lost it!"

"Lost it?"

"The machine ate it."

"Ate it!"

"It's just gone. Lost. Gone!"

Gladys and Maude stand at their typewriters, raise their arms, and cheer.

We no longer fear that computers will steal our jobs. Today, we download a Request for Proposal off the Internet, keyboard the draft directly into computers, revise it forty-seven times on-line, and rush it out by overnight courier late the night before it's due. NASA and the National Science Foundation now require us to post our proposals directly to their Web sites. We e-mail proposals to Japan, and they are received halfway around the world before we have a chance to find that crucial error. We stay open to change.

> ## Where Did This Writer Go Wrong?
>
> Spotted in the preface of a proposal:
>
> *Too late for inclusion in this proposal, an error has been discovered.*
>
> God knows they *tried* to get them all in.

## ACCEPT. LET BE.

A young English boy living in India asked his amah, "Why are you always so happy? What is the secret?" She answered, "Accept. Let be." In a world of constant change and confusion, we will never understand it all. To write proposals serenely, just accept. Let be.

By the 1990s, computer technology has become commonplace, but the zany atmosphere goes on. I try to print a proposal from California to our Washington office late at night so they can deliver it to the client by noon the next day. The printer I choose has been turned off. Easy. I choose a different printer. Halfway through printing, the printer in Washington runs out of paper. I can't add paper three thousand miles away, so I set the timer to print early the next morning. But whose time zone should I set it for: my computer's time zone in California or the printer's time zone in Washington? In Zen tradition, I think: *Not one, not two.* I serenely set it for both times, leave voice mail messages for Washington, and go home to bed.

First thing in the morning, I call the Washington office. "Did you get it?"

"Oh, honey, the first time, the printer ran out of toner. Sheets and sheets of blurry gray stuff."

"But the second printing?"

"Coming out just fine. We'll get it there with, oh, ten minutes to spare."

See? Don't worry, be happy. Accept. Let be. I find I must learn this lesson anew with each proposal. But then, relearning it helps me keep my beginner's mind.

●

## KEEPING YOUR BEGINNER'S MIND

You can learn to enjoy the perils of proposals. When you start to become frantic, take a deep breath and let it out slowly. Remind yourself:

- Keep your beginner's mind, open to learning something new.
- Stay open to change and new experiences.
- Accept. Let be. What's the worst that could happen?

> The way you know you're having an adventure is when you wish you were home in bed.
>
> —MARK TWAIN

# One Hand Clapping

## 3

## THE SOUND WE MAKE WHEN WE FORGET TO CONNECT
## WITH OUR READERS

*Your audience is one single reader. I have found that sometimes it helps to pick out one person—a real person you know, or an imagined person—and write to that one.*

—JOHN STEINBECK

In some Zen groups, students are taught to meditate by just focusing on their breathing and letting the mind be empty. In other Zen groups, the Zen Master assigns a koan to the student, who goes off to meditate on it. More than a thousand Zen koans exist. They don't have right answers because they are not riddles. They are also not paradoxes designed to shock the Zen student. They can be anything: a question, a word from a Zen story, or a moment from the life of an ancient Master. By meditating on this koan, the student is expected to gain a direct realization of basic reality, or what Alan Watts describes as "a clear, unobstructed mind into which he can toss the koan like a pebble into a pool and simply watch to see what his mind does with it."

Like a Zen Master, I will ask you many questions in this chapter. I will also assign you a koan. Here it is:

Who is my reader?

Ask yourself this question constantly as you plan and write a proposal. Are you writing this proposal for yourself? No, you're writing it for your reader, your client, the buyer. Your objective is to help the reader understand what you're trying to say. All the other questions in this chapter are variations on this koan: Who is my reader?

Let's look at the difficulties of connecting with the people who will read your proposal. Do you recognize having any of these thoughts as you plan a proposal?

- Is my idea any good, anyway?
- What do I want to say?
- Can I actually write this?
- What's the best way for me to say it?
- How can I convince anyone to buy this idea?
- What do I want to say first?
- How do I want to organize this proposal?
- What do I mean to say here?

These seem like legitimate questions, but the focus is wrong. You're thinking only about yourself, your needs, your doubts, and your wants. Your fears. Let's turn it upside down and start thinking about the reader, the reviewer, the evaluator, the editor—in short, the buyer. If we do, the questions change.

| FROM | TO |
| --- | --- |
| Is my idea any good, anyway? | Who will want to buy this idea? |
| What do I want to say? | What does the buyer want to hear? |
| Can I actually write this? | How can I target my idea to this specific buyer? |
| What's the best way for me to say it? | How will that buyer understand it best? |
| How can I convince anyone to buy this idea? | What logic or persuasion or entertainment will attract that buyer? |
| What do I want to say first? | What will this buyer want to know first? |
| How do I want to organize this proposal? | What will the buyer want to know next? |
| What do I mean to say here? | What does this buyer need to hear at this point to be convinced? |

See the difference? Now that you're not worrying about yourself, you can plan your proposal to pinpoint the needs of that buyer. Now the *pressure* is on the buyer/reader.

In one of my first workshops on writing proposals, we did an exercise to identify our reader. We talked a lot about this reader. I even made a little form to be filled out.

Your Reader's Name:_____

Your Reader's Title: _____

What is this person's expertise? _____

What power does this person have? _____

During the workshop, I walked around the room looking over people's shoulders while they were writing. After reading for a minute, I always asked, "Who is your reader?" Once I leaned over the shoulder of an engineer and asked: "Who is your reader?" He looked up and said, "You are." Whoa, this is true. In the workshop, I am their ultimate reader. So I learned to expand the questions on the form to cover all the readers:

What is your original face before your mother and father were born?

—ZEN KOAN

Who are my readers?

—YOUR KOAN

- Who are your first readers?
- Who are your second readers?
- Which reader has the authority to sign the check?

## WHO ARE YOUR FIRST READERS?

Stop reading now and decide who is the first reader for the proposal you are writing. Write down everything you know about this person: name, title, expertise, position of power. Now imagine this person reading your proposal in the ideal setting: a quiet book-lined study with a fire in the fireplace or a spacious office with the phone permanently on hold. All the time in the world to read and savor your proposal, right? Wrong.

No matter how perceptive this reader, he or she will be reading your proposal under appalling conditions. Reviewers read proposals in addition to their regular work, and they are all just as busy as you are. If they have an urgent problem to solve during the day at work—and they always do—they take the proposals home with them and read them on the commuter train.

> How old would you be if you didn't know how old you was?
> —Satchel Paige
>
> Who is my first reader?
> —Your koan

## First Readers of Business and Government Proposals

A proposal reviewer for an investment company says your first reader should be your spouse:

> Write your idea on a single sheet of paper, double-spaced. Give it to your spouse to read after ten-thirty P.M., when he or she is very tired and the heat is turned up. Let your spouse read it for only fifteen minutes. Then ask for a first impression.

Max Yoder, who reviewed proposals for the Chief of Naval Research for thirty years, starts the introduction to his brochure, "The R&D Proposal: Putting Your Best Ideas Forward and Avoiding the Pitfalls," like this:

> In my thirty years of proposal reviewing for the Chief of Naval Research, I simply have not thoroughly mastered (to my satisfaction) the art of determining the intent of a poorly written proposal. Of the literally many hundreds of proposals evaluated, I have found them boring, exhilarating, perplexing, profound, disorganized, highly meritorious, and a few not worth the paper they were written upon. After reviewing research and development proposals from universities, small businesses, nonprofit corporations, and major business corporations, I have determined that I am reaching a point of diminishing returns—extrasensory perception continues to elude me.

A reviewer for environmental grants warned against trying to disguise a poorly developed idea with lots of obvious smoke screens:

If you can't make your point in the first page or two, the likelihood that an evaluator is going to have the fortitude to dig through all the smoke and find the essence is pretty small.

What all these readers are saying is, they can't read your mind. First, make sure you understand your own idea. Then make it clear. Keep it simple.

## First Readers of Book Proposals

In book publishing, the acquisition editors are always pushed. They already have four-foot stacks of manuscripts on their desks, and your book proposal will just add to their workload.

At the California Writers Club Conference at Asilomar in June 1995, the keynote speaker was John Baker, editor of *Publishers Weekly*. He talked about the early days of book publishing, when publishers and senior editors were sons born into wealthy families. They didn't want to become bankers or lawyers, so they majored in literature at Yale and Harvard and went into publishing. The bright young women they hired straight out of Radcliffe, Sweet Briar, and Smith were the readers of the slush pile—that mountain of manuscripts that grew each day as the mail was opened. Occasionally, these young women found a great book in the slush.

Book publishing, said Baker, is now run by large companies (primarily companies outside the United States) in the business to make money. Many book publishers are now intent on the blockbuster novel, the big book by the celebrity, and the book that is sure to make a large return on investment. Gone are the wealthy editors who had the grace and time to help new writers along, encouraging them, suggesting ideas. Today, publishers depend on the agents to do their first screening.

Even the agents don't read all the book proposals. They will give your proposal to both amateur and professional readers. The first reader of your book proposal will probably be a person who just likes to read good books (maybe the agent's spouse). Your second first reader will be a person who knows books professionally. This reader will be more critical. If you make it through these two readers and they like the ideas in your proposal, they'll recommend that the agent read it. So when your agent calls you long distance and says, "We loved it," he really means *we*.

## Choosing Your First Readers

Instead of relying on chance, you can choose your own first readers. Here are some of the people I asked to read my draft of the proposal for this book:

- Chris, who markets research, has a 100 percent hit rate on proposals, and loves reading good books.
- Michael, who edits professionally for business writers and collects Japanese art.
- Marlys, a writing teacher and Esalen counselor, who has published a successful college textbook.
- Kevin, who routinely writes proposals in his job and was born knowing how to convince people to give him money.

Each person gave me brilliant ideas that made the proposal far better than my draft. Check your network of colleagues, friends, and family to find people who will tell you honestly what they think.

## If Your First Reader Is Your Boss

If you're writing a proposal at your company, your first reader is probably your manager. What if your writing styles don't match? Some managers are excellent editors, but people in my workshops often complain that they write something as clearly as they can and then their managers fuzzy it all up.

This is reality, and this is hard. Breathing and meditation won't make the problem go away, but these steps can make it better:

> A girl is crossing the street.
> Is she the younger or the older sister?
>
> —Zen koan
>
> Who are my second readers?
>
> —Your koan

- Find out if your style of writing really *is* clear. Take a workshop on writing, and try to get your manager into the workshop with you.
- Be sure your style is appropriate. A proposal to the National Science Foundation is expected to be more formal than a proposal to a book editor or a business client.

- Talk to your manager about style and tone *before* you start writing. Read some of your manager's writing to get a feel for his or her style.
- Read chapter 10 on how to stay serene when writing on a team.

## WHO ARE YOUR SECOND READERS?

Even your second readers don't have to read the proposal from beginning to end. The University of Michigan did a survey of one thousand managers and top executives to ask them how they read the proposals and reports that came across their desks.

- Only 3 percent of them ever read a report or proposal straight through.
- They *all* read the summary if there was one and perhaps the introduction. Then they skipped to the conclusion.
- If costs were presented, 90 percent of them read the cost section.
- If they liked what they read, they delegated review of the other sections to others.

While editing proposals to the government, I always visualized the proposal reviewers being impressed with the well-structured flow of our prose. I assumed they would be so caught up in our proposal, they could not help but read it from beginning to end. But no. Frank, who has been winning research contracts on atmospheric pollution for over thirty years, brings us news from a reviewer of government proposals.

This guy who just reviewed our proposal told me how it works. First, they are handed a pile of proposals that made it through the first screening. They are also given a list of evaluation criteria and told to score each proposal points according to the criteria.

This reviewer's technique was to read several proposals at once. He said, "I start with the first evaluation criterion, read that section of four or five proposals, and score them all for that criterion. Then I take the next criterion and score all proposals on that one." He almost never reads any one proposal straight through. If he can't find the section that tells him what he needs to know to assign a score, it's just too bad.

Max Yoder, who reviewed proposals for the Chief of Naval Research, echoes this advice:

> If the reviewer becomes accustomed to looking in a certain section of the proposal for a certain detail and your proposal does not have such a detail in that place, it may be overlooked. Even worse . . . the proposal could be disqualified altogether if a prescribed format is not followed.

## WHICH READER CAN SIGN THE CHECK?

In the early 1990s, Lee Buchanan was director of the Technology Reinvestment Program (TRP), a government program that had $250 million to assign to people who could convert military technology to commercial uses and make new jobs to help heal the economy. The TRP received three thousand proposals the first year of the program. Buchanan said:

> Take pity on the beleaguered evaluators, who will be faced with stacks of proposals and just six weeks to divvy up the $250 million allocated for the competition. If a proposal is not written in readily comprehensible English, you have made the evaluator work so hard, the evaluator is not even going to get through it—and that happens a lot.

A reported asked Spencer Tracy what advice he would give to aspiring movie actors. Tracy said, "Learn your lines and hit your marks."

Who is my ultimate reader?

—YOUR KOAN

Buchanan said the secret was to write clearly and follow the printed rules. He was amazed at how many people invented new rules and included letters from their governors, senators, and congressmen and were then very upset when their proposals didn't win.

Proposal evaluators are instructed to disregard all the irrelevant materials offered, but that's hard. It's like asking a jury to ignore the very exciting testimony they just heard. If a proposal contains a lot of irrelevant stuff, an evaluator may decide those things have been put in because of a lack of substance—as filler.

But if it's not in the proposal, they also can't rate it. When I was working on this book at Asilomar, a retreat by the sea near Monterey, California, I met a charming couple who had come down to Asilomar to get away from an unusual heat wave in the San Francisco Bay Area. The husband worked as a subcontract administrator for a big defense supplier and routinely reviewed proposals from would-be subcontractors. He said:

> If it doesn't appear in the proposal, I can't give them credit. Once I had to turn down a proposal from a friend of mine for that reason. The guy called me up, pretty upset, and said, "You know we can do the job, Bob. Why did you reject my proposal?" I had to tell him that the proposal just didn't say what it needed to prove it.

Do *anything* you can to make it easier for this final, crucial reader to understand your unique idea. You want to lay it out so clearly that even a tired, busy, distracted, bored reader will

- read it easily.
- get the concept.
- think it's great.
- send money.

But how do you know what they want to buy? How do you get inside your reviewer's mind, and how do you write to that mind? That's what we're going to work on in the next chapter. First, here are some simple reminders and exercises.

## SIMPLE WAYS TO CONNECT WITH YOUR READER

Now that we understand how proposal reviewers read and under what conditions, how does that change the way we need to write? Here are some simple ways to connect with your reviewers:

- Read and follow the instructions. Really. Write the proposal exactly the way the client asks you to write it.

- Use lots of headings to catch the reviewer's eye. Break up those long sections.
- Revive that classic idea of the topic sentence to tell them exactly what you're going to say in that paragraph.
- Realize that proposal reviewers at government agencies such as the National Institutes of Health are often people for whom English is a second language. Don't confuse them with sentence structures like "be that as it may" or words like "albeit."
- Never distract the reviewer with typos or grammatical errors.
- Think about how you feel when you have to work so hard to understand what some writer is trying to say. Write simply, so you don't put your reader through this pain.

### Exercises for Getting to Know Your Readers

First, who is your ultimate reader? Jot down three things this person most wants to know or do. For example, he wants to know how to _____. Or she wants to be able to _____.

Now, who are your other readers? Imagine them as tangibly as you can. Start with your first readers and move up to the reader who can sign the check: the senior editor or the technical reviewer at the government agency or the CEO of the company you are selling to. Write down their names and titles and answer the questions in the boxes below. If you don't know their names, get on the Internet and find out who they are or just describe their positions.

---

Your First Reader's Name: _____

This Reader's Title: _____

What is this person's expertise? _____

What power does this person have? _____

What does this reader need to see to pass your proposal on to the person above? _____

_____

---

Your Second Reader's Name: _____

This Reader's Title: _____

What is this person's expertise? _____

What power does this person have? _____

What does this reader need to see to pass your proposal on to the person above? _____

Your Final Reader's Name: _____

This Reader's Title: _____

What is this person's expertise? _____

What power does this person have? _____

What problem does this person have that your proposal will solve?

_____

If you're writing a book proposal, you also need to visualize the readers who will hand over their credit cards in the bookstore. In *How to Write and Sell Your First Nonfiction Book,* Oscar Collier and Frances S. Leighton recommend that you write down all the things you cannot know about these readers but think may be true. What TV programs do these readers watch? What music do they listen to? What magazines do they read? Where do they buy books? What kinds of books? Do they watch football games or listen to opera on Sunday afternoons? What journals do they read? Do they play chess or tennis? In short, get to know your audience.

Your assigned koan is "Who is my reader?" Meditate on it constantly as you write. If you get very tired of this koan, try another one: "How can I help my reader understand?"

# Not Two

## WHAT ARE YOU TRYING TO SELL? WHAT DOES YOUR CLIENT WANT TO BUY?

*When you sit in the full lotus position, your left foot is on your right thigh and your right foot is on your left thigh. When we cross our legs like this, even though we have a right leg and a left leg, they have become one. The position expresses the oneness of duality: not two and not one. This is the most important teaching: not two and not one. Our body and mind are not two and not one. If you think your body and mind are two, that is wrong; if you think that they are one, that is also wrong. Our body and mind are both two and one.*

—SHUNRYU SUZUKI

Like our body and mind, what you're selling and what your client is buying are not the same. But because sales do happen, they're also not different. This chapter helps you become comfortable with the idea that your needs and your client's needs are not two and not one. It shows you how to sell your wonderful idea without compromising it.

To sell your idea in a winning proposal:

Write about what the client wants to buy, not just about what you want to sell.

Sounds like a Zen koan, but it's not. It's simple, good advice. Here's an example. When my son graduated from high school, I helped him buy a car. We agreed it would be a used car, reasonably priced but safe. He found a Bronco. Safe, which was what I wanted, and macho, which was what he wanted. He took it out for a drive all that first afternoon.

The next morning, I found this note on the refrigerator, scrawled on a piece of lined paper torn from his spiral binder:

> Dear Mom,
>     Thank you, thank you for the Bronco! Only one problem. My Scout leader says the tires are too worn to be safe. I need to buy new ones, and big ones are best. Since you own half the car, would you buy two of the tires? I'll buy the other two when I save enough from my job at the pizza place.
>     But that could mean I'd still have two unsafe tires for at least 6 months. Will you also advance me the money for the other two tires? I promise to pay you back from my pizza money. If you agree, I can be driving on safe tires right away.
>
> Your most grateful son

When we talked that evening, I agreed. The next morning, I woke up thinking, *Good heavens, I agreed to spring for four brand-new tires. How did he get me to agree to that?* Because he wrote his proposal about an idea I wanted to buy (safety), not just the idea he wanted to sell (flashy new tires).

For another example, let's go back to that first proposal many of us wrote—the letter from summer camp. In *The Making of the Atomic Bomb*, Richard Rhodes tells about the early life of Robert Oppenheimer:

> Robert was a carefully brought up boy in a select, carefully controlled environment. When he was fourteen, to get him out of doors and perhaps to help him find friends, his parents sent him to camp. . . . He was shy, awkward, unbearably precious, and condescending. . . . He wrote his parents that he was glad to be at camp because he was learning the facts of life. The Oppenheimers came running.

Oppenheimer certainly sparked action in his readers. Why? Because he appealed to their needs rather than his own.

Do I mean you should abandon your principles and sell only what the market is buying? No, I mean you should target your proposal to appeal to the client's needs, not just your needs. You will still write your proposal about your wonderful, unique, useful idea, but from your client's point of view.

How do you know what your client wants to buy? How do you know your client's needs? First, which audience are you selling to? What kind of buyer will be interested in your idea?

In a series of workshops we did on client-centered marketing, Ed Claussen, the head of our training department, came up with these ideas to help people determine the real needs of their clients:

You must always be a good date for your reader.

—KURT VONNEGUT

> You need to determine the real needs of clients so you can address those needs in a way that differentiates you from their other choices. You need to help clients see how the potential payoff from your proposed idea will more than justify the needed investment.

Ed said that one way to describe your idea is in terms of its technical features—how it works. But a better way is to translate those features into benefits so that clients can easily understand how your idea can solve their problems. If you can get them to see the benefits, you can sell the idea. First, you need to figure out the benefits of your idea, and to do that, you need to ask yourself lots of questions.

First, what do business clients care about? They care about results. They care about

- solving their pressing problems.
- improving their revenues and profit margins.
- enhancing their product line.
- reducing their cycle times for development and delivery.
- improving quality.
- gaining a sustainable advantage over their competitors.
- avoiding catastrophes.

Come to think of it, book publishers care about most of these same things, don't they?

Now you need to answer these questions:

What am I selling?
Who will buy it?
Why will they buy it?

## WHAT AM I SELLING?

Ed Claussen made up what he calls the " 'So what?' diagram" as a way of understanding exactly what we are selling. Here's an example of a "So what?" diagram for a product one company marketed very successfully:

*Offering:*        A proprietary ink formulation for industrial and office printers.

*Features:*        Water-fast, water-based.

*So What?*        The ink won't run if the paper gets wet. Needs no toxic solvent.

*So What?*        Significant improvement over non-water-fast inks now used in office inkjet printers.
Could replace the toxic solvent-based inks used in industrial inkjet printers.

*So What?*        Exclusive license gives manufacturer a competitive advantage.
Less expensive to produce.
Manufacturer's production staff and printer operators don't have to breathe toxic fumes or clean up toxic material.

*Tangible Value:*  Projected impact on industrial sales: $10 million to $20 million/year.
Projected profits: $2 million to $4 million/year.
Projected payback on investment: Recovery in 2 months.

This diagram will work for any kind of idea. On the first line, you summarize your idea. Let's say it's a new source of energy. You will probably say why it's important to *you* here, but that's a good start. On the second line, give the specific features of your idea. For example, it can harness the methane from seventeen pounds of bird droppings to run a twelve-volt battery for two hours.

Go to the third line and answer the question "So what?" What's important about this idea of yours? Why should someone who can sign the check care about it? Don't stop with your first reason. During the gas shortage in the 1970s, every proposal I read that had anything at all to do with energy said that this idea would "relieve the gas shortage." One proposal said:

At the same time we face the reality of tightening energy reserves, society is also awakening to the specter of uncontrolled pollution and has taken positive steps to ensure that such pollution shall not exist.

I shuddered at this specter.

Today, any proposal related to energy says the idea will "reduce the dependence on foreign sources of petroleum." You've got to do better than that. *How* will it reduce dependence on foreign oil sources? How *much* will it reduce it? *Why* is it a better source of energy than oil? How *much* cheaper will it make energy? Is it safe? Is it environmentally sound?

Keep answering the question "So what?" until you can state clearly and simply the benefits of this idea to a client. Some of these benefits will lead you naturally to the tangible value, the financial value of the idea.

## WHO WILL BUY IT?

Now that you know what could be important to a client about your idea, you can start looking for specific buyers. Who has a problem this idea will solve? What kinds of workers would benefit from this product or idea?

You can find buyers on the Internet, or you can scan the newspaper called the *Commerce Business Daily*, which describes what the government wants to buy. Every day, page after page lists needs—from toothbrushes to jet planes to research. Each government agency also publishes lists of what it wants to buy, usually in the form of Broad Agency Announcements (BAAs). These BAAs list the problems that an agency needs to solve, describes the kinds of solutions it is looking for, and tells you how to apply for funding to solve this problem.

Both the government and business clients also put out Requests for Proposals. These RFPs set out a well-defined Statement of Work, specifying what tasks the client wants you to perform, and tell you exactly how the client wants the proposal written.

Chris Peterson, who works in program development for a research company, says:

Ten years ago, if you didn't know about the RFP before it came out, you had only a one in twenty chance of winning. Today, the odds are much worse.

How do you find out ahead of time? You visit your clients. You write and send e-mails and call them. Ideally, you want to be in such close contact with your clients that they will tell you about their next RFP. They may even send you a draft of the RFP, and at this point you have a chance of influencing what it covers. The perfect situation is that you get to help write the Statement of Work.

What if you don't yet have that kind of contact with your clients? Go to their Web sites and look at their current RFPs and BAAs. These will give you the names, phone numbers, and e-mail addresses of the people you need to get to know. And they encourage you to get in touch and tell them your ideas. Send them a short concept paper. They may well say it's too late for *this* RFP, "but we've got another one coming out in six months that really fits with your idea."

You can also start with a client's need—what they want to buy—then develop your idea. Subhash Narang, the head of a polymer chemistry research group, regularly reads the business section of the *San Francisco Chronicle* for ideas. One day he saw an article on the need to recycle old used tires. Most of the known methods cost too much because they required grinding up the tires, and they didn't use up enough tires. A California agency was interested in funding good ideas for recycling tires. Another article in that same business section talked about the need to make buildings resistant to microwave radiation, especially buildings containing advanced computers. Subhash put the two needs together and got a sizable grant for incorporating hunks of old tires into the walls of buildings to deflect microwaves.

## WHY WILL THEY BUY IT?

You've defined what you're selling, and you've identified who will buy it. Now you need to work on the next question: Why will they buy it? The one right answer is: Because it solves their problem. Therefore:

> The single most important thing your proposal must do is convince the client that your idea solves their problem.

> The "So what?" diagrams help you clarify the benefits of your idea. Now you need to clearly state these benefits in your proposal. Where in the proposal?

Certainly not on page thirty-two. On page one. You'd be surprised how often proposal writers forget to do this.

MASTER EDITOR: How will your idea solve their problem?

PROPOSAL WRITER: It's obvious.

MASTER EDITOR: Tell me anyway.

PROPOSAL WRITER: Well, if our idea works, it would meet their need for a more powerful, longer-lasting, lightweight energy source. And it would be environmentally friendly. It would cost less than what they're using now, and it would be a no-brainer to operate.

MASTER EDITOR: Good, let's say that in the proposal.

PROPOSAL WRITER: But it's already *in* there.

MASTER EDITOR: Exactly where?

PROPOSAL WRITER: (thumbing through the proposal) I know it's here. (flips ahead) Somewhere. (flips back) Here, here it is! Page seventeen. Had a little trouble finding it.

MASTER EDITOR: Let's move it up front, okay?

If you have even a *little* trouble finding the solutions to your client's problem, the reviewers will *never* find them. Remember, the reviewers are tired, rushed, distracted, sleepy, and probably bored with the whole idea of reading other people's proposals. They want to get back to writing their own proposals. You need to catch their attention early.

One time, our company had an idea for helping a major chemical company eliminate ammonia from its industry processing waste streams. Our idea was scientifically sound, and it was innovative. It also took advantage of our advanced computer program that could accurately compute the savings to the company from *any* changes in its waste streams.

All that helped, but here's what cinched the sale: Our idea would not only eliminate ammonia from the waste streams, it would allow the chemical company to then turn around and *sell* the ammonia, making a *profit* for the company from this previous nuisance waste. In the first draft of the proposal, this idea was on page fourteen of a fifteen-page proposal. We moved it to page one and won a $1 million prize.

## NOT TWO AND NOT ONE

To sell your idea, you need to reconcile what you're trying to sell with what your client wants to buy. They are not two and not one. You can find out where they overlap by pinpointing the benefits of your idea to a client and matching those benefits to a client's needs. Then, write your proposal about what your client wants to buy, not about what you want to sell.

### EXERCISE

Use the "So what?" diagram to explore your idea. Then write one paragraph that shows the client clearly and specifically how your idea will solve their problem.

*Offering:* _____
_____

*Features:* _____
_____

*So What?* _____
_____
_____

*So What?* _____
_____
_____

*So What?* _____
_____
_____

*Tangible Value:* _____
_____
_____

# The Tea Ceremony Is a Ritual of Precision

## DON'T FIGHT THE FORMAT

*The art of the Way of Tea consists simply of boiling water, preparing tea, and drinking it.*

—RIKYU

The Way of Tea sounds like total simplicity, doesn't it? However, the following description, from Kakuzo Okakura's *The Book of Tea*, shows the tea ceremony as complex. In the manner of Zen, both can be true.

> The host will not enter the tearoom until all the guests have seated themselves and quiet reigns with nothing to break the silence save the note of the boiling water in the iron kettle. The kettle sings well, for pieces of iron are so arranged in the bottom as to produce a peculiar melody in which one may hear the echoes of a cataract muffled by clouds, of a distant sea breaking among the rocks, a rainstorm sweeping through a bamboo forest, or of the soughing of pines on some faraway hill.

In the ceremony of proposal writing, the rituals are just as precise as in the Japanese tea ceremony. Some proposal requirements are simple; some are complex. And as in the Zen tea ceremony, these formalities have a practical purpose. Do not think of proposal guidelines as hobbling. Think of them as a ritual, a soothing ritual to be followed to reach enlightened funding.

## THE RITUALS OF TEA DRINKING

The Japanese tea ceremony is a Zen way of contemplating beauty and simplicity through formality. Each part of the tea ceremony has precise but simple steps that foster tranquillity. The tearoom itself is designed to avoid the appearance of perfection. In *The Book of Tea*, Okakura said that the Zen idea of beauty "can be discovered only by one who mentally completes the incomplete. . . . It is left to each guest in imagination to complete the total effect in relation to himself." For this reason, the design of the tearoom avoids symmetry and uniformity of design. Okakura describes how even the tearoom decorations must be planned so that no color or design is repeated:

> If you have a living flower, a painting of flowers is not allowable. If you are using a round kettle, the water pitcher should be angular. A cup with a black glaze should not be associated with a tea-caddy of black lacquer. In placing a vase on an incense burner on the tokonoma, care should be taken not to put it in the exact centre, lest it divide the space into equal halves.

What a complex system for achieving simplicity.

When my younger sister and I were teaching at a high school in Japan, one of the students, Nobuko, invited us to a tea ceremony. She met us that day dressed in kimono, rather than her dark school uniform, and took us to a small building with simple wooden walls set in a garden of stones and pines. The room was spare and subdued. The only decoration was a single spray of white plum blossoms in an alcove. We sat watching while Nobuko explained the steps to us.

The woman preparing the tea wore a brown kimono, her waist encircled by a dull orange obi. In slow, graceful movements, she put the water on to boil in a metal kettle. All her movements were slow and stylized, but one struck me especially. When she reached out her right arm to take the kettle off the fire, her left hand, with fingers held straight, moved gracefully under her elbow to hold back the sleeve of her kimono. It seemed like one step in a slow dance.

When she handed me my cup of tea, she held it out in both hands. Nobuko spoke quietly: "Take the bowl in both hands because it is an important gift. Now bow to the tea server. No, don't drink yet. First, you must admire the tea bowl. Turn it one-quarter turn." The bowl was of rough pottery with a dull blue glaze that left parts of the clay irregularly exposed. The randomness made the glaze even more beautiful. "Good," said Nobuko. "Now bow again and take one sip." I did exactly as she said, and my reward was a drink of dusty green tea that puckered my mouth.

Months later, I was wearing a light cotton kimono (*yukata*) at home and reached out to pour myself a cup of coffee. As one hand reached over the stove for the coffeepot, my other hand moved under my elbow to hold back the *yukata* sleeve. It startled me. What I had thought was part of a stylized dance was simply a natural, "right action" for a person wearing kimono.

Zen sneaks up on you like that.

## THE RITUALS OF PROPOSAL WRITING

Proposal writing has its own rituals. For proposals to the government, the guide to the ritual is called the Request for Proposal (the RFP). In book publishing, it is called the Book Proposal, and for magazine articles and genre book publishing, it is the Publisher's Guidelines. These ritual guidelines tell you exactly how that potential buyer wants the proposal written—how long it should be, what it should cover, how it should sit on the page. Everything.

Here's an example from a U.S. government RFP:

Volume I, Technical Proposal, shall not exceed thirty (30) pages, including the required cover sheet, all figures, references, tables, charts, and appendices. All proposals must be double-spaced on paper not greater than 8.5 by 11 inches in size and typed single-sided with 1.0 inch minimum top, bottom, and side margins. The font size must not be smaller than 12 point. Separate attachments such as institutional brochures, reprints, or videotapes will be ignored.

Brilliant people will immediately figure out a way to get around these rules. After all, that's what brilliant people are good at—thinking beyond the boundaries. They will debate the precise meaning of "double-spaced." They will decide to squeeze the space between paragraphs. Hey, why have paragraphs at all? Just run it all together. They will end up meeting the picky-picky requirements but producing an unreadable mass of type for the proposal reviewers.

The easy way to follow these format rules is to grasp the concept:

They want a short proposal.

Therefore, the easy way is to write a short proposal. Don't try to give them a long proposal disguised as a short one. The reviewers will not be fooled, and they will resent such tricks.

The easy way is the Zen way: Don't fight the format; simply accept the ritual. Let's look first at what can be the simplest ritual—the proposal to a commercial business—and work our way up in complexity through the book proposal to the proposal to a government agency.

## THE COMMERCIAL PROPOSAL

The only hard rule for a proposal to a commercial business is KISS: Keep It Short and Simple (also known as Keep It Simple, Stupid). This kind of proposal should just need to close the deal because you've already met with the client, you've already learned what problem they need to solve, and you've already told them your ideas for solving their problem. You've agreed on the general plan of work, and if you've done it right, you've also persuaded the client to let you write the Statement of Work. You also know who can make the final decision and sign the check.

Here's all you need to do in a formal proposal to a business:

> Don't use your proposal as a vehicle to introduce new ideas to the customer. It is far too late at that stage. You should have done that when the customer first started thinking about what to put in the RFP.
> —Dick Close

- Show you really understand their problem.
- Tell them your ideas for solving their problem (perhaps holding back enough so they can't do it themselves).
- Show them how much better off they'll be after you solve their problem.
- Tell them what it costs.
- Give them something to sign.

If they don't sign right away, you may need to talk to them some more. You may need to revise the proposal according to their questions or suggestions. But that's really great: now you have the client writing the proposal for you!

## THE BOOK PROPOSAL

A book proposal is a way to help the editor buy your book without actually having to read it. And for a nonfiction book, you can use the book proposal to sell your book before actually having to write it. The basic book proposal needs to answer the following questions:

What's the book about?
Why should *you* be the one to write it?
What's the market for this book (who will buy it)?
How is it different from all those other books?
What form will it take?

You need to answer these questions in about ten double-spaced pages (publishers want *everything* double-spaced). The first page is most important because it needs to summarize the answers to all the questions. The first paragraph is crucial because you must capture their attention fast before they go on to read all the other proposals stacked up on their desks.

The Manuscript Marketplace of the Maui Writers Conference allows you to submit a two-page "manuscript résumé," which the conference will forward to over a hundred agents and editors. Their first instruction for this résumé is about the book concept: "Describe your book in one to three sentences." They advise you to spend some time writing and rewriting this "pitch line" to capture the heart of the book. Here's the pitch line for Sam Horn's book, *Tongue Fu!*:

Martial arts for the mind and mouth that help us deal with difficult individuals without becoming one ourselves.

Book proposals can be written in many forms and styles to match the styles of the books they are selling. For some good examples and more details, read any of the books listed under "Writing Book Proposals" in Other Resources at the end of this book. I recommend starting with a book by Jeff Herman and Deborah M. Adams called *Write the Perfect Book Proposal: 10 Proposals That Sold and Why.*

## THE GOVERNMENT PROPOSAL

In Zen gardens, the stone walkways over ponds have jogs in them so that powerful spirits will misstep and fall into the water. Government Requests for Proposals can be an inch-thick stack of paper with all the crucial instructions hidden and tucked away among endless pages of governmentese. I think these RFPs are meant to be a maze to trap those spirits not zealous enough to make it through.

Once, a government RFP gave a page limit of 298 pages. Now that was just asking for trouble. Everyone was going to write 298 pages whether they needed to or not. The only thing we could figure was that they already had one 298-page proposal they wanted to fund, so they used that as the page limit.

The first time an RFP had a strict page limit, one of our proposal writers called Chris, the head of marketing, and said, "The editor says the proposal can't be longer than ten pages."

"What does the RFP say?" Chris asked.

"Well, it says ten pages, but I can't believe they really mean it."

Chris said, "Why would they lie?"

Larry Dubois, formerly head of a section at the Defense Advanced Research Projects Agency, said:

> The most important thing in writing a government proposal is to read the RFP and follow the instructions.

Sounds as simple as Zen, but if you don't read the whole RFP carefully, you may miss that *one sentence* that says you can't bid unless you're a university or unless you share 50 percent of the cost. One of my jobs as a technical editor was to read the RFPs, then summarize the important requirements and make detailed outlines for the proposal writers. (*Someone* has to read it all, and the scientists are usually happy to read just the Statement of Work, then go off to figure out the science part of it.)

If it's a typical government RFP, say, from the Department of Defense or the Department of Energy, the first sections will tell you the agency's overall objectives and what they are generally looking to buy in this RFP. Section J (Sections A through I, if they ever existed, appear to have been abandoned) says it will give you the attachments. However, it really gives you only a list of attachments and you must flounder around to find them elsewhere in the stack of paper. One of the attachments will be the Statement of Work, if there is one—precisely what tasks they want you to bid on.

> Answer the customer's problem. If he wanted a different problem solved, he would have asked for that. Don't surprise him. Surprises get your bid thrown out as nonresponsive.
>
> —DICK CLOSE

Section K includes the representations and certifications (contractual forms about equal employment opportunities, lobbying, and other standard government regulations). Section L gives detailed instructions on the format and content of the proposal—now we're getting somewhere. Some of the stuff that should be in Section L (like where to mail it and how many copies) will instead be sequestered in other sections. Section M gives the evaluation criteria.

Like the pain-pleasure of easing yourself into a too-hot bath, I grew to enjoy the challenge of finding what we needed in all this itemized and decimal-numbered stuff. At first, it took me two full days to read and outline an RFP. To speed things up, I developed the following simple template for the RFP summary and a streamlining method called "Pin-Stitch-and-Iron."

## THE PIN-STITCH-AND-IRON METHOD FOR OUTLINING RFPS

When I was in the fifth grade, we were taught to sew by making an apron. We couldn't just sit down and sew it. We had to pin the pieces of cloth together, baste the seam, take out the pins, and iron the seam. Then we were allowed to stitch the seam, take out the basting, and iron again. It took us six months to finish the apron. My mother, a very practical woman, said this was nonsense: "Just pin, stitch, and iron and you're done." I used that same simple approach for summarizing RFPs.

Client:
Source: [publication or Web site]
RFP Number:
Title:

**Objectives:**

**Deliverables:** [reports, samples, prototypes]

**Contractual/Costing:** [type of contract, duration, level of effort, special costing requirements, cost sharing, forms]

**Proposal Format:** [number of volumes, page limit, special forms, packaging requirements]

Proposals are due by [time and date]. Send 1 original and [XX] copies to

**Pin:** Take five minutes to flip through the RFP to get a feel for its organization (and make sure you have it all).

Use paper clips to separate any sections you know you won't need to read *in detail*, such as Section K, the representations and certifications.

Take thirty minutes to underline, mark the margin, or label relevant sections with sticky notes as you go. You're not studying for a test, just locating the information you need. (Don't use a highlighter, because it will copy solid black over the words when someone asks for a copy of the RFP.)

**Stitch:** Take about two hours to input your summary and outline. The *slow* way to do this is to try to fill in the template linearly from top to bottom. Fill in the objectives, then search through the RFP for the reporting requirements, then search again through the RFP for all the contractual issues, and so on.

The quick way is to *turn the RFP pages only once.* On the first page, you will probably find the RFP number, title, and due date. Fill these in on the template wherever they go. Turn the next page of the RFP and add to the template any information the template calls for. Keep going straight through the RFP, just throwing information into the appropriate sections of the template without worrying about order or continuity or grammar or spelling.

Complete the proposal outline from the Section L (instructions) first, then blend in any requirements from Section M (evaluation criteria).

When you reach the last page of the RFP, your template contains all the information needed.

**Iron:** Take about forty-five minutes to edit your summary, moving sentences around to pull together related subjects. Condense information from several sentences into one newspaper-style sentence to keep the summary to one page.

Check the facts in the summary and check the outline against Sections L and M. Do a spelling check, and print.

You will now have an "apron" in less than three hours!

The end of this chapter gives an expanded template with reminder questions to help you read and outline an RFP, then a sample one-page summary for a real RFP from the Department of Energy. This summary would be followed by a detailed outline of the proposal contents and evaluation criteria.

## EXPANDED RFP TEMPLATE:

Client:
Source: [publication or Web site]
RFP Number:
Title:

**Objective:** [Does the RFP list general areas of interest, or is there a specific Statement of Work? Any restrictions on who is eligible to bid? Do they encourage teaming of universities, industry, and government labs?]

**Deliverables:** [What types of reports, samples, or prototypes need to be delivered? When are they due? How many copies? Do you need to travel for review meetings?]

**Contractual/Costing:** [Will the agency make multiple awards or a single award? What type of award: grant, cooperative agreement, contract (fixed price, cost-plus-fixed-fee, level of effort, time and materials)? Does the RFP require that you share in the cost? How much? Cash or in-kind (labor, materials)? How much money is available? What will average funding be? For how long? Is a level of effort specified? How much detail do they want in the cost estimates (total only, by year, by fiscal year, by task)?]

**Proposal Format:** [How many volumes do they want? What are the page limits? Any restrictions on format (font size, characters per inch, single- or double-spaced, page size, margins)? Are any special forms required? How do they want it presented (staple, comb bind, in binders, other)? How do they want it packaged? What markings are required on the package?]
   [How do they want the proposal structured? What topics need to be included? What are the evaluation criteria? How will they score it?]
   [How do they want it sent (by mail, by courier, by e-mail, on disk, to their Web site)? If electronic, what platform and software? If paper, how many copies?]
   Proposals are due by [time and date]. Send one original and [how many?] copies to [what address? Does the site have restrictions on access?].

## SAMPLE SUMMARY OF A GOVERNMENT REQUEST FOR PROPOSAL

Client: Department of Energy, Federal Energy Technology Center (FETC)
Source: http://www.fetc.doe.gov/business/solicit/
Financial Assistance Solicitation number DE-PS26-99FT40578
Title: Department of Technologies and Analytical Capabilities for Vision 21 Energy Plants

**Objective:** The goal of Vision 21 is to eliminate all environmental concerns about using fossil fuels for producing electricity, transportation fuels, and high-value chemicals by building high-efficiency, low-emission fossil fuel plants. The objective of this solicitation is to develop the capabilities needed for these Vision 21 plants. Attachment A gives examples of technologies of interest within these areas. DOE encourages **teaming** of industry with other kinds of organizations. At least 75% of the direct labor costs should be incurred in the United States.

**Deliverables:** Technical Progress Report, Topical Reports (as required), and a Final Report (draft final due 30 days after end of project; approved final due 90 days after end of project).

**Contractual/Costing:** FETC plans to award 10 to 15 Cooperative Agreements for up to 3 years. Budget includes $5 million to $10 million in each of 3 years FY00, FY01, and FY02. The **minimum cost share is 20 percent.** See Section II.B for unallowable cost sharing. Use April 30, 2000, as start date. Proposals must be valid for 180 days. Costing requires detailed budget, using DOE form 4600.4 for industry or form 4620.1 for a university.

**Proposal Format:** The proposal must be in two volumes:

| VOLUME | TITLE | ORIGINAL | COPIES | ELECTRONIC VERSION |
|---|---|---|---|---|
| I | Business and Financial Application | 1 | 2 | 1 |
| II | Technical Application | 1 | 4 | 1* |

*The electronic version of the technical application must be submitted in WordPerfect 6.1 or Adobe Acrobat portable document format (PDF).

Volume II is limited to **50 single-spaced pages.** Section II.W gives notice to protect proprietary information. On each page, give the name of the applicant, date, and the solicitation number. All forms required for the proposal are given in WordPerfect 6.1.

Proposals are due by **2:00 P.M., November 30, 1999.** Send proposal to

U.S. Department of Energy / Federal Energy Technology Center
Attn: Raymond D. Johnson
Wallace Road [we'll need a street address for FedEx]
P.O. Box 10940, MS 921-107 / Pittsburgh, PA 15236-0940

**Packaging:** Wrap the originals of all volumes and the 2 copies of Volume I as one package. Wrap all copies of Volume II as a separate package. Mark the outside of each package with the solicitation number, program Area of Interest, and the volumes in the package.

# Experience Beyond Thought

## THREE WAYS TO BRAINSTORM NEW IDEAS OR ENRICH OLD ONES

*"Drink a cup of tea," as they say in Zen. Don't think about drinking a cup of tea—just drink it. Taste it. Feel it. Enjoy it. That is experience beyond thought.*
—DIANA ST. RUTH

In the last chapter, we talked about accepting the rituals and restrictions of proposal writing. Here, we'll look at ways of *freeing* ourselves from restrictions—ways of experiencing our ideas without thought. Brainstorming is one way to release new ideas freely and quickly without judging or trying to organize them. It's a way to wake up your creative mind so that it explodes with fresh ideas.

## MEDITATION AS A STIMULANT

Meditation is often seen as a way of soothing and quieting ourselves. It can be that, of course, but it's also a way of waking ourselves up. In *Sitting: A Guide to Buddhist Meditation,* Diana St. Ruth says that meditation "is similar to arousing ourselves from a very deep sleep . . . a process of freeing the mind of its entanglements, of learning how to undo the knot."

Meditation can help us become fully awake and fully aware of everything we experience. St. Ruth writes:

Awareness is the key. But what does the word mean? To most people, perhaps, it denotes an acknowledgment of that which is going on around them in a general sort of way. In the context of meditation, however, it means "waking up," becoming acutely sensitive, knowing, feeling, living the moment in its pristine state, sensing colors and contours, sounds, textures, smells. It means recognizing tendencies within oneself yet resisting the pull to be controlled by them. This is meditation—to begin with at least.

How can we use this type of awareness to help us experience our new ideas before we can censor them with thought?

## HOW DO YOU USUALLY THINK AND LEARN?

We can't stop thinking entirely, but we can change our patterns of thinking. First, it helps if you know how you usually think, how you prefer to learn. Are you primarily visual, aural, spatial, or kinetic? For example, I think and learn almost entirely visually. To remember someone's name, I need to *see* it. If I don't get the person's card, I go away quickly and write down the name. It is almost impossible for me to learn something new by hearing it. Don't *tell* me how to get to your house: write it down. And if you ask me to follow your car, I'll surely get lost.

To discover how you prefer to think and learn, take this short quiz. It's not a serious analysis, just a way to observe yourself. For each question, choose the one answer that most closely fits your needs.

### How Do I Usually Think and Learn?

1. If I am going to your house for a party and I've never been there before, I'd prefer to find my way by asking you to
   a. write down the directions.
   b. tell me how to get there (go three miles south, turn left at the stop light, go three blocks west).
   c. draw me a map.
   d. let me follow your car.

2. To learn a new physical task, such as driving a car or operating a computer, I prefer to
   a. read the manual.
   b. have someone tell me how to do it.
   c. watch someone else do it.
   d. try it for myself.
3. To remind myself to bring an object to work, I
   a. post a note on my refrigerator.
   b. ask a household member to remind me.
   c. put the object in front of the door.
   d. carry the object out to the car.
4. To memorize a speech, I prefer to
   a. write it out word for word and read it over and over.
   b. record it and listen to it.
   c. type the speech on three-by-five cards and spread them out on a large surface.
   d. stand up and give the speech to a mirror, using gestures.

With only four questions, this quiz is hardly scientific. It's simply a way to see if you have a strong preference for one or two patterns of thinking and learning.

- If you chose mostly item a [visual], you like to learn by seeing things.
- If you picked more of item b [aural], you learn best by hearing.
- Many item c [spatial] answers shows that you remember things by their spatial orientation—where they are.
- Item d [kinetic] shows you learn by doing—by moving your body or the object.

For brainstorming, you want to purposely shift to different thinking/learning modes to loosen up your mind and stimulate creative thinking. As the Apple ads say:

Think Different.

For example, if you generally use visual techniques for learning or thinking, you'll loosen up faster in brainstorming if you try working in another mode such as spatial or kinetic. If you're brainstorming in a group, you want to give everyone a chance to expand their ways of thinking by incorporating all four types of thinking patterns.

## BRAINSTORMING AS STIMULANT

Brainstorming is certainly not the same as meditating, but the techniques are similar because in both you need to

- isolate yourself from the distractions of the world.
- focus on this single, particular moment.
- avoid thinking or directing your thoughts.

> If I plunge my hands into steaming hot water, I don't need to think about whether the water is hot or not! I don't need to tell myself, "Oh, I've scalded my hands."
> —Diana St. Ruth

When we have a thought during meditation, we let it drift away. When we have an idea during brainstorming, we don't evaluate it or judge it to see if it's a *good* idea. It's an idea. Accept it without thought.

Brainstorming is meant to be spontaneous and creative, but most of us need some stimulation to keep us in that mode. We tend to analyze and critique ideas immediately and look for problems before proceeding further. If you are brainstorming alone, here are some ways to keep it free:

Work quickly without stopping.
Record everything just as it comes.
Don't judge your ideas.
Don't worry about repetition.
Don't worry about grammar, spelling, and punctuation.
Don't organize your ideas [yet].

If you are brainstorming in a group, it helps to remind people:

Any idea is okay.

All criticism will be postponed.

Repetition is fine.

One idea can build on another.

Often, when brainstorming in a group, everyone sits still while one person records the ideas. Why not open it up? Let people rush up to write down an idea. Let people wander around the room or lie down on the floor. You could also link your group on a computer network and allow everyone to add their ideas to the link.

Brainstorming is a way to unlock our minds, to allow them to play. Here are three ways to experience new ideas by opening your thinking patterns to new and different paths:

1. Releasing words into the air.
2. Mindmapping.
3. Stickies.

## Releasing Words into the Air

To release words into the air, we're going to play with key words. Not sentences, not even phrases, unless they come naturally. Just freely release words from your mind. You can write them down (visual), dictate them onto a tape (aural), or keyboard them into your computer (kinetic). The trick is to keep your creative brain awake and free, to allow yourself to play.

At a writers conference, I was celebrating a book deal with my agents while dancing to loud music performed by the Cliff Notes. Like the band called the Rock Bottom Remainders, this group was made up of best-selling authors, including Ridley Pearson, Dave Barry, and Mitch Albom. More than one hundred people were dancing wildly. It must have been during an encore of "Twist and Shout" that I strained a muscle in my knee. The next morning, I had to hold on to the wall to walk at all.

Sitting with my ice-packed leg up on the chaise longue, I could see the headline: WRITER CONFINED TO LUXURY HOTEL ROOM. Hey, this was not all bad. I snagged my notebook and spent the afternoon brainstorming thirty-seven ways to combat the fear of public speaking. It didn't matter if the ideas were good or silly, because this was just a way to while away a lovely afternoon in a fine hotel. Those notes, edited down, became a chapter in this book.

In *Zen in the Art of Writing,* Ray Bradbury described a similar experience:

> In my early twenties I floundered into a word-association process in which I simply got out of bed each morning, walked to my desk, and put down any word or series of words that happened along in my head.
>
> I would then take arms against the word, or for it, and bring on an assortment of characters to weigh the word and show me its meaning in my own life. An hour or two hours later, to my amazement, a new story would be finished and done. The surprise was total and lovely.

What I did that afternoon in the hotel room was the simplest form of brainstorming: Soothe yourself into an open, freewheeling mood and write down all the words that come into your head. To go a step further, and free yourself from even *words,* try the next technique.

## Mindmapping

Mindmapping is a spatial and visual technique developed by Joyce Wycoff and described in the book *Mindmapping: Your Personal Guide to Exploring Creativity and Problem-Solving.* It's like releasing words into the air, except you draw pictures and symbols to represent your ideas. Wycoff encourages using images and symbols as "a shorthand to the brain," which is what Zen calls "experience beyond thought." You draw these picture ideas on whiteboards or large sheets of paper taped up around the room, so anyone can add an idea anywhere at any time.

Many people find this method difficult because they are so attuned to working with words. In my workshops, I've found I must first forbid people to talk to each other or to write notes. Finally, in a burst of the need to communicate, they begin to draw pictures.

In one workshop, the brainstorming assignment was to find new uses for a paint NASA had developed for protecting the gantries at Cape Canaveral from the extreme heat of the rocket exhausts and from coastal spray and fog. This paint was special because it didn't buckle at high temperatures, and it prevented rust and deterioration for many years. However, the paint was also very expensive to manufacture. How could this technology be transferred to the public sector? Who would make the paint? Who could afford to buy it?

Mindmapping was slow at first: sketches of the sun, the ocean, and paintbrushes. Then one person drew a patio table and barbecue. Another drew a beach umbrella. (Possible uses for the paint?) Someone else quickly drew a big dollar sign and a question mark. (Is this paint too expensive for the backyard market?) Another drew a dollar sign with an arrow running down from it to a question mark. (Can we lower the cost?) By drawing pictures and symbols, they worked on the problem. Finally, someone drew a light bulb (corny symbols are just fine) and a sketch of the Eiffel Tower. Immediately, someone else drew a suspension bridge. Others drew the Golden Gate, the Brooklyn Bridge, and the London Bridge! (Ah, the paint could be used for large-scale public structures such as bridges. Here, the high cost of the paint wouldn't matter because it would save the high labor costs of continually repainting the structures.)

In mindmapping, you end up with pictures of your ideas. As you see ideas that branch off one idea, you can draw arrows or circles linking one idea to another. You can also give each person a different color marker so each can identify his or her ideas later.

## Stickies

In the stickies technique, you release both words and images, but you put them on sticky paper tags like Post-it® Notes and stick them all over a whiteboard or large sheets of paper. The stickies method combines visual, spatial, and kinetic modes of thinking. You can add the aural mode if you encourage people to shout out their ideas as they write them down. Get a variety of sizes and colors of stickies to experience your ideas in 3D and Technicolor.

## TRYING IT TOGETHER

Let's try an example of brainstorming together now to see how you can carry it further. Your manager has asked you to recommend a site for the company's next off-site meeting. You are asked to present your ideas orally at a staff meeting, then follow up with a written proposal. You and your audience have different objectives:

- Your manager wants to hold a productive meeting that promotes teamwork while controlling the cost.
- Your co-workers want to get out of the office and have a good time.
- You want a free vacation in Hawaii.

Where do you start? By playing with the idea.

Use any of the three techniques previously described to capture all the ideas that come to mind about having an off-site meeting in Hawaii. You may end up with a mishmash of ideas like this (if you're mindmapping or using stickies, you'll also have images and symbols):

| | | |
|---|---|---|
| White sandy beach | Quiet setting | Away from crowds, tourists |
| Serenity | Low costs | Snorkeling |
| Low stress | Airline discounts | Surfing |
| Zen meditation | Hotel discounts for large group | Camp on Na Pali coast |
| Plumeria blossoms | Rent whole house at beach | Research cost/site on Internet |
| Coconut palms and banyan trees and coral sands | Free food for staff | Papayas, pineapple, mangoes, guavas, ahi, ono, mahimahi |
| Healthful food | Free bikes | Health spa |
| Yoga classes | Tai chi in mornings | Low cost to staff as well as company |
| Rent Charo's villa on Kauai | | Sunsets |
| Sunrise | Zen retreat on Maui | Stress-free |
| No distractions | Soothing music | |
| Screaming room | Conference room outdoors | Meet on the beach |
| Spa resort | Remote site | |
| Not tourist center | Not expensive | Camp on beach |
| Stress-free | Low key | Comfortable clothes |
| No shoes | Mai tais | Scuba dives |
| Orchids and tiny umbrellas | Piña coladas | Sashimi |
| Pupu platters | | Frequent flyer miles |
| Sarongs | Bikinis | Tans/sunscreen |
| Waterfalls | Helicopter tour of Na Pali | Quiet |
| Humahumanukunukuapuaa | Rest and work | Bali Hai |

Some of these ideas are silly and some are useful, but they are *ideas*. Now let's group these random ideas into categories. For this first step, don't eliminate any ideas and don't worry about overlapping ideas or repetition. We'll rank them later. For now, just get them into categories.

Recalling the priorities and needs of your manager and co-workers, we could set up these categories and fit the ideas under them. If you are using the stickies method, you can simply move them around. Use big stickies for the headings. For mindmapping, use different-colored circles to link ideas.

| CONDUCIVE TO PRODUCTIVITY | COST CONTROL | SITE ADVANTAGES |
| --- | --- | --- |
| Serenity | Low costs | Healthful food |
| Low stress | Airline discounts | Not tourist center |
| No distractions | Hotel discounts for large group | No shoes |
| Stress-free/stress-free | Free food for staff | Comfortable clothes |
| Quiet setting | Not expensive | Conference rooms outdoors |
| Rest and work | Internet research | Low key |
| Quiet | Low cost to staff as well as company | Away from crowds, tourists |
| Remote site | Frequent flyer miles | Meet on the beach |

| PLEASURES AVAILABLE | LODGING CHOICES | POSSIBLE ACTIVITIES |
| --- | --- | --- |
| White sandy beach | Rent Charo's villa on Kauai | Zen meditation |
| Plumeria blossoms | Spa resort | Yoga classes |
| Coconut palms and banyan trees and coral sands | Rent whole house at beach | Screaming room |
| Sunrise/sunset | | Pupu platters |
| Orchids and tiny umbrellas | Zen retreat on Maui | Hike to waterfalls |
| Sarongs | Camp on Na Pali coast | Free bikes |
| Bikinis | Health spa | Tai chi in mornings |
| Humahumanukunukuapuaa | | Soothing music |
| Mai tais | Camp on beach | Helicopter tour of Na Pali |
| Piña coladas | | Snorkeling |
| | | Surfing |
| Papayas, pineapple, mangoes, guavas, ahi, ono, mahimahi | | Scuba dives |
| Sashimi | | Tans/sunscreen |
| Bali Hai | | |

A certain order is emerging, isn't it? Some ideas are realistic and useful. Some are delightful daydreams. Let's rank them now as to importance and priority. Importance to your audience: your manager and co-workers. Under each heading, mark a ranking of 1 to 10 for each idea. It's okay if several ideas are marked 1, meaning most important. You can sort them again later. Ideas marked 10 are ideas you are probably not going to use.

Again, for the stickies technique, you can simply move your stickies into a different order. For mindmapping, use colors to rate ideas. You could make red most important, through the colors of the rainbow to violet, least important.

Under the six headings, we might decide that the following ideas are most important. You can now eliminate silly ideas. You will also come up with some new ideas, such as the cost-control advantages of many of the activities.

| | |
|---|---|
| *Conducive to Productivity* | No distractions |
| | Ability to both rest and work |
| | A quiet, low-stress, serene environment |
| *Cost Control* | Airline discounts for large group |
| | Optional use of frequent flyer miles |
| | Lodging discount for large group |
| | Prepare our own food |
| | Low cost to staff as well as company |
| *Lodging/Site Recommendation* | Rent large house on Kauai north shore |
| | Book the whole Zen retreat on Maui |
| | Get discounted condos at remote resort on Kauai |
| *Site Advantages* | Low-key setting away from crowds, tourists |
| | Relaxed atmosphere: comfortable clothes, no shoes |
| | Outdoor meetings possible |
| | Healthful surroundings: food, quiet, beauty |
| *Low-Cost Activities* | Meditation, yoga, tai chi, sunrise/sunset |
| | Beach walking, hiking, snorkeling, Hawaiian music |
| | No-host receptions |
| *Optional Activities* | Scuba, surfing, helicopter tours, plumeria leis on arrival |

You can almost write your opening sentence now, can't you? Something like the following:

I recommend a site for our next off-site staff meeting that is conducive to productivity, low cost to both staff and the company, and provides a relaxed, healthful setting.

Don't do it yet, though. First, we need to get organized.

## EXPERIENCE BEYOND THOUGHT

Use brainstorming, like meditation, to wake yourself up. Be fully aware so that you can experience new ideas without pondering them. Be brave in brainstorming! Be thunderstruck! Who knows where you're going? Charge ahead to experience your new ideas without thought.

# CHOP WOOD, CARRY WATER

Sit Down and Start It

# From Clutter to Simplicity

SETTING A PATH FOR YOUR PROPOSAL

*1. Out of clutter, find simplicity.*

*2. From discord, find harmony.*

*3. In the middle of difficulty lies opportunity.*

—EINSTEIN'S three rules of work

At some point, you need to build a structure for your proposal, even if it's only a flimsy, temporary pup tent. But hey, Zen is all about *not* getting organized, *not* planning the future. Just living in the now. So why are we worrying about setting a path? Why do we need structure?

The student asked the Zen Master, "How can I get off this tiresome wheel of sleeping, eating, and washing?" The Zen Master answered, "Sleep, eat, wash." Setting a path for your proposal is a way of being mindful of one piece of it at a time, like simply sleeping or simply eating or simply washing. Setting a path will free you from the distraction of thinking about the whole proposal at once.

## YOU'VE ALREADY STARTED

The secret is, you've done most of the structuring already in the process of imagining your readers. We've talked about the initial planning stage, where you figure out what your reader (client or reviewer) cares about most. You jotted down three things your reader most wants to know. And you decided what you want to persuade your reader to do. You've brainstormed your ideas and have a big, clumsy, disordered pile of ideas you want to cover.

Now you need to draw on that knowledge of your readers and simplify the ideas you've collected to set up a temporary structure for your proposal. The key word here is "temporary." You can—and will—change this structure when you start writing. Let it guide you, but not restrict you.

Chapter 3 listed some of the questions people ask themselves when they start to prepare a proposal and how they can get stuck by worrying about what they are going to say. We saw how we can relieve the pressure by turning the questions upside down to stop thinking about ourselves and to think about the buyer. When we change our focus, the questions change from the worrying questions on the left to the planning questions on the right.

| WORRYING | PLANNING |
|---|---|
| Is my idea any good, anyway? | Who will want to buy this idea? |
| What do I want to say? | What does the buyer want to hear? |
| What's the best way for me to say it? | How will that buyer best understand it? |
| How can I convince anyone to buy this idea? | What logic or persuasion or entertainment will attract that buyer? |
| What do I want to say first? | What will this buyer want to know first? |
| How do I want to organize this proposal? | What will the buyer want to know next? |
| What do I mean to say here? | What does this buyer need to hear at this point to be convinced? |
| Can I actually write this? | How can I target my idea to this specific buyer? |

You have already used these questions to clarify what you are selling and who wants to buy it. You have practiced aiming your proposal toward your reader's interests and needs. Now, the *structure* of your proposal is going to come from the questions in the right-hand column. You can already begin to organize your proposal by answering the questions:

- What does this buyer want to know first?
- What next?
- What does the buyer need to know to be convinced?

In the previous chapter, we played with ways to develop new ideas freely and quickly, without judging them. Now that we're all in a freewheeling, right-brained mode, why not just stay in that mode? Isn't it more Zen-like to just start writing without any planning or organizing?

No. Zen is about being mindful—being fully focused on the event or task at hand. Winging it may *seem* more creative, but the writing will probably take you three times longer. If you write without some kind of path to follow, you can spend hours wandering around writing sections you won't use. You can set off in all directions and have to start over when you realize what you intended to say. You can get lost and discouraged. You can also get right up to your deadline before finding you've left out some crucial ideas. But there will be no more time!

If you organize first, the creativity can—and will—come while you're drafting the proposal. If you create even a temporary framework, you can relax within that frame.

## YOU DON'T NEED A DETAILED OUTLINE

I'm not talking about the rigid, detailed outline Miss Whitehead made you do in the fifth grade:

    I. INTRODUCTION
        A. Premise
            1. First Point
            2. Second Point
                a. Picky parts of second point
                b. Other picky details
        B. Background

I never could make that kind of outline until *after* I had written the assignment. I'm simply talking about grouping and ranking your ideas to create a general structure. Remember, you're not locked in: you can always change the structure as you write.

This structure can actually be comforting. Imagine driving south over the Golden Gate Bridge to San Francisco. It's a gorgeous day, and the bay is full of sailboats. The city lies white and sparkling before you. You are driving on a bridge suspended by cables hundreds of feet above the water. When the wind blows, the bridge swings slightly beneath your car. In a small car, you can be shifted into another lane by the wind. Now imagine you're at the midpoint of the bridge before you realize they've removed the guardrails on each side of the bridge. Are you still having fun?

The boundary of the path you set for your proposal will free you from the distractions of worrying about where you're going.

## BUILDING A TEMPORARY STRUCTURE

What do these temporary structures look like? Here are some examples that have worked for many writers.

### Just List Your Topics

George, a mechanical engineer, told me how he and his thesis adviser set about organizing his thesis. He and the professor first drew up a list of topics that should be covered. The professor assigned George to write one or two sentences under each topic—just to state the core of the idea. Once he had those sentences, they met again to decide on the *order* of these topics. That list was the outline. And those sentences eventually became the topic sentences for each section of the thesis.

### Sort Your Brainstormed Ideas

If you've brainstormed many new ideas, sort these ideas into categories, as we discussed in chapter 6. Set priorities for these ideas and eliminate those with little or no priority. Sort them again into what seems like a logical sequence for your reader. This sequence becomes your outline.

### Draw Pictures

Make spatial diagrams to show your priority ranking of your ideas. These can be circles tied together with spokes or branches that fan out from a central idea, like a tree. They can be visual hierarchies with ladders of points under them, somewhat like sentence diagrams. Use any form that gives you a visual picture of the structure for your proposal.

Go to www.thinkingmaps.com, the Web site for the Innovative Learning Group, to view many ways a visual outline can be structured. Click on Software to download exercises to play around with.

### Make a Storyboard

A storyboard combines the visual structure described above with a verbal structure. For complex proposals to be written by a team, some companies make up a storyboard for each section of the proposal. This form gives the written outline for that section (and the client's evaluation criteria), the winning strategy for that idea, and rough sketches of the figures and tables that are expected. Topic sentences are given for each part of the section. The writers take their storyboards and go off and write their sections, which are reviewed and approved by the team leaders as the proposal progresses.

### Follow Convention

A comfortable way of getting organized for many writers is to start with what's been done before. The typical grant proposal is as structured as a formal dance. It's usually set up like this:

| | |
|---|---|
| *Executive Summary* | A short summary of your ideas and their benefits to the client. |
| *Objective* | What you hope to achieve. |
| *Background* | What work has been done before and why a new approach is needed. |
| *Proposed Approach* | How *you* plan to tackle the problem and why your approach shows such promise. |
| *Statement of Work* | A bulleted list of precisely what tasks you propose to perform. |
| *Personnel* | Why you and your people are the best for this job. |
| *Facilities* | A description of the equipment and facilities available for this work. |

| | |
|---|---|
| *Budget* | What this work will cost. |
| *References* | Citations to the literature on this topic. |

This outline is really bare bones, but it's a clear beginning. If nothing else, it will help you separate your objectives from your approach and *your* approach from the work that has been done before. Max Yoder, a reviewer of proposals for the Chief of Naval Research, says:

> A sure way to befuddle the reviewer is to have a section entitled "Background and Technical Approach." This will invariably ensure that the reviewer will have great difficulty in determining just what part it is of all the things you described that *you* are actually proposing to accomplish. . . . *Always* separate out *your* technical approach from the mass of background information and all other possible approaches to the problem.

You'll need to set some structure within these sections to keep you on track, but you're on your way to a clear proposal.

## WHEN THE CLIENT HAS ALREADY SET THE STRUCTURE

Frank, an atmospheric scientist, organizes his proposals right down the line of the evaluation criteria in the Request for Proposals. Each section and each paragraph starts with a response to a specific evaluation criterion. "It's not great literature," he says, "but it wins contracts."

Earlier, we looked at some of the expectations and requirements for proposals. Proposals solicited by the government must usually follow the outline given in the Request for Proposals. Not much need to organize here, just start filling in the blanks in the outline.

Book proposals are pretty much organized around the information an agent or editor wants to know:

What's the book about?
Why should *you* be the one to write it?
What's the market for this book (who will buy it)?
How is it different from all those other books?
What form will it take?

Proposals to business clients are written after you've spent a lot of time talking to the client and organizing the proposals together. In the formal proposal to a business, you just need to

- show you really understand their problem (or their needs).
- tell them your ideas for solving their problem (or meeting their needs).
- show them how much better off they'll be after you solve their problem.
- tell them what it costs.
- give them something to sign.

If your client has already set the structure, just follow it.

## SETTING A PATH

Before you begin to write that proposal, you need to simplify the clutter of ideas in your mind. Forget about that dreaded idea of "outlining" and simply focus your ideas so that you can be mindful of one piece at a time, free of the distraction of worrying about the whole.

> If you have built castles in the air, your work need not be lost; that is where they should be. Now put the foundations under them.
>
> —HENRY DAVID THOREAU

# Zazen Meditation

## HOW TO WRITE THAT PROPOSAL IN SPITE OF YOURSELF

*What is called* zazen *is sitting on a pillow in a quiet room, absolutely still, in the exact and proper position, and without uttering a word, the mind empty of any thought, good or wicked. It is continuing to sit peacefully, facing a wall, and nothing more. Every day.*

—Taisen Deshimaru

If you are trying to write a proposal, I don't have to tell you about *zazen*—sitting meditation. You already know all about sitting and staring at the blank white paper. Or sitting in front of your computer, gazing at the mandala of your screen saver.

But sitting without writing is like meditating without breathing. You must do *something. And* you must not expect to achieve anything.

When I was in the fourth grade, my older sister devised a new club that my younger sister and I might join. The initiation ritual was to stand in a corner for three minutes and *not* think of a white bear. Because we also had to be honest, we never got in the club. That's what we're going to do here: try *not* to write that proposal. But it must be specifically *that proposal* we are avoiding.

We all know how to avoid work. To avoid cleaning the house or paying bills, I simply avoid doing anything else. I call it "fusting," a wonderful old word Shakespeare used in *Hamlet:*

> . . . What is a man,
> If his chief good and market of his time
> Be but to sleep and feed? A beast, no more.
> Sure he that made us with such large discourse

Looking before and after, gave us not
That capability and godlike reason
To fust in us unus'd.

My theory of fusting is: If I'm not sitting down, I'm not doing anything. Therefore, I'm not avoiding the work I should be doing. I stand on the deck in the sun, drinking coffee. I stand in front of the open refrigerator, eating without sitting. I stand at the bathroom mirror, practicing raising one eyebrow. As long as I'm standing, I'm almost ready to start the work. Any minute now.

I can fust easily for two hours. With concentration, for three. But with a proposal to write, fusting will not do. Here, we are not just avoiding work, not just avoiding writing. We are avoiding writing *that proposal*.

You know the ordinary ways to avoid writing:

- Checking your mail, e-mail, voice mail, fax machine.
- Rearranging all your files.
- Surfing the Internet.
- Changing your screen saver.
- Phoning the dentist.

After all, maybe you don't *have* to write this proposal. Maybe you can find some way out of it. If not, you must breathe deeply and focus on not writing it, just as in meditation you focus on not thinking. Here are some simple Zen steps.

## STEP 1: WHEN YOU FUST, JUST FUST

Enjoy fusting. Be mindful of whatever you are doing. Feel the pebbled smoothness of an orange. Smell it. Lick it. Peel it and be mindful of the feel of white pith under your fingernails. Put only half a section in your mouth and relish it.

Thich Nhat Hanh wrote about being mindful this way:

While washing the dishes one should only be washing the dishes, which means that while washing the dishes one should be completely aware of the fact that one is washing the dishes. At first glance, that might seem a little silly: why put so much stress on a simple thing? But that's precisely the point. The fact that I am standing there and washing these bowls is a wondrous reality. I'm being completely myself, following my breath, conscious of my presence, and conscious of my thoughts and actions. There's no way I can be tossed around mindlessly like a bottle slapped here and there on the waves.

> In walking, just walk.
> In sitting, just sit. Above all, don't wobble.
>
> —YUN-MEN

Or you can simply change your screen saver with mindful grace.

## STEP 2: SIT DOWN

My five-year-old grandson comes into my room and tells me he cannot sleep. "Of course you can't sleep, sweet-face, you're standing up. Go back and lie down." He hates that advice.

Most of us need to sit down to write, just as we need to lie down to sleep. One writer who didn't sit down was Thomas Wolfe (Thomas of *Look Homeward, Angel*, not Tom of *Bonfire of the Vanities*, although neither one had any problem pouring out words). Thomas Wolfe, a tall man with a short refrigerator, stood and wrote by hand on top of his refrigerator in Brooklyn. He turned out manuscripts that he hauled into his editor's office in packing crates. Several square yards of words would be hewed down to six-hundred-page books by his editor, Maxwell Perkins.

Wolfe's neighbor tells of hearing Wolfe walking along under his window at three in the morning, chanting: "I wrote ten thousand words today, I wrote ten thousand words today, I wrote ten thousand words today."

Only the rare bird can write standing up. Sit down.

> Writing is easy; all you do is sit staring at a blank sheet of paper until the drops of blood form on your forehead.
>
> —GENE FOWLER

## STEP 3: PICK UP YOUR PENCIL, OR TURN ON YOUR COMPUTER

> I write many thousands of words a day, and some of them go on paper.
> —JOHN STEINBECK

When I am avoiding writing, I pace around the room thinking I am writing until I see the computer screen dark. I now have a sign on the wall that reads, "Turn It On!"

Gail Godwin, the author of nine novels including *A Mother and Two Daughters*, tells of climbing the stairs to her study with dread, then turning on her computer and being "amazingly cheered by its booting-up noises . . . sweet, hopeful, familiar blumps and beeps."

## STEP 4: WRITE SOMETHING ELSE

When I am trying to avoid writing a proposal, I sit at my computer, staring at the screen. Not writing. If I sit there not writing long enough, the screen saver shows me a teapot that tries to shoot down flying saucers. When the teapot hits a saucer, there is a loud and pleasing sound of smashing crockery. The teapot flips its lid and does a little dance of pleasure. I wait for the teapot to hit just one more saucer. Then I will write.

So: Write something else. Your goal is to prevent the screen saver from telling the people in the next room that you are not writing.

Steinbeck went to his studio every weekday morning and wrote a long letter to his editor on the left-hand pages of a notebook in which the facing pages would be filled with the text of his novel. He wrote about how badly he had slept the night before, or his worries about his sons, or about seeing *The King and I* on Broadway. He said it was his way of "getting my mental arm in shape to pitch a good game."

Most often he obsessed about his pencils:

For years I have looked for the perfect pencil. I have found very good ones but never the perfect one. And all the time it was not the pencils but me.

A pencil that is all right some days is no good another day. For example, yesterday, I used a special pencil soft and fine and it floated over the paper just wonderfully. So this morning I try the same kind. And they crack on me. Points break and all hell is let loose. This is the day when I am stabbing the paper.

> I love being a writer. What I can't stand is the paperwork.
> —Peter De Vries

Now that's what I call writing something else.

Steinbeck then went on to write for four hours, or about 1,500 words a day (rarely on weekends), until he finished the 567-page book called *East of Eden*.

Sue Grafton, who writes the "alphabet" mysteries *(A Is for Alibi, B Is for Burglar . . .)* and is working her way through to Z, starts each day keyboarding her feelings into a journal. That shifts gradually into thinking about scenes in the book she's having trouble with. When she's ready, she goes into the file for that chapter of the book.

So, do a warm-up. You do it before you run or play tennis. Why not for writing?

One way to warm up is just to type up your notes into a clear form. A retired race car driver was covering a big race for *Playboy* magazine. *Playboy* had offered its usual high payment and had promoted the story widely. The deadline for the article came and went, but the writer was still "working on it." Finally, the editor at *Playboy* suggested that the race car driver pass his notes on to another writer. "But the way I take my notes, they won't make sense to anyone but me." The wise editor then suggested that the driver just type up his notes clearly for the other writer. The driver set to work eagerly, and within a day he had written the article *Playboy* published.

A variation on writing something else is called "automatic writing." Just keep those fingers moving over the keyboard. Retype your previous paragraph or write yourself a note about how you're stuck and why you're stuck. Keep on writing until your fingers resign themselves to staying in motion for the four hours or one hour or half hour you have set for this task.

You may get so bored with writing nonsense that you might just as well write *that proposal*.

## STEP 5: SKIP TO WHAT'S EASY TO WRITE

When I edit proposals, I usually find that the summary and the introduction need lots of editing. Once the writer gets to the meat of the thing, it begins to hang together. The writing is less stilted, more natural. It goes.

But starting is hard. Steinbeck wrote this in his notebook:

I suffer as always from the fear of putting down the first line. It is amazing the terrors, the magics, the prayers, the straightening shyness that assails one. It is as though the words were not only indelible but that they spread out like dye in water and color everything around them.

So write the easy part first. Write the routine sections first or the sections you know best how to write. If you get stuck on a hard section, skip to an easy one. Save the introduction for last. Is this chicken? Sure, but you will eventually write the introduction, just as your child will eventually become potty trained. All books have introductions, and very few graduating seniors walk down the aisle wearing diapers.

Know that you will write it all. Just not today.

## STEP 6: SET YOUR WRITING HOURS OR WORD QUOTA

Ray, manager of a successful company for fifteen years, set aside half an hour first thing each morning to write his proposals. "The trick was," he said, "I started writing six months before the proposal was due."

Don't even think about writing the whole proposal. Set a specific amount of time you will write each day, whether it's four hours or one hour. Then sit and write for that time even if what you're writing seems worthless.

Or set your word quota. Set the number of words you will write each day. Whether it's 1,000 words or 300, keep writing until you have that many words on paper. A typewritten, double-spaced page is about 250 words, so 1,000 words is about four typewritten pages. On my computer, a double-spaced page in twelve-point

Times font is about 300 words. Most word-processing programs will count the words for you. When you get stuck, but you know you need to write only 173 more words, you'll keep going.

## STEP 7: STOP WHEN THE GOING'S GOOD

Thomas Mann said the best time to stop writing is when you know exactly what will happen next. When you've met your time or word quota for the day and you know exactly what to write next, discipline your-self to stop. Jot some notes for tomorrow. I promise you'll start off with a bang in the morning.

The people in my workshops *never* buy this idea. The cautious person in the front row says, "Let me be sure I understand. You want me to stop writing just when I'm rolling?"

"Yes. After you've written for the length of time you promised yourself or the number of words, stop."

"But I'll forget all the good stuff."

"I don't think you will."

"Can I just make a few notes?"

"Sure, make notes."

"Then stop?"

"Yes. When you start to write the next day, it'll be easy to pick up where you left off because you'll know where you're going."

The reckless person in the back of the room says, "Excuse me, but I think that's just a pretty dumb idea."

"Okay, keep on writing until you run out of anything to say."

"Until I'm stuck."

"Exactly."

"Sounds good to me," he says.

"And what will you be feeling the next time you sit down to write?"

"Stuck?"

"Stuck."

Nobody in my workshops ever thinks this is a good idea. Until they try it.

> Jack London wrote only one thousand words a day, but he did it *every* day, whether he was on the high seas or hung over in Tahiti. He published forty-four books.

Let's look at the math. You write until you run out of steam and you have written 2,000 words. Next day, you're too tired to write at all, and on the third day, you write only 500 words because it took so long to get going.

| Day 1: | 2,000 words |
|---|---|
| Day 2: | 0 words |
| Day 3: | 500 words |
| Total: | 2,500 words |

If you'd written 1,000 words a day, you'd have 3,000 words. A difference of 500 words may not sound like much, but by the end of thirty days, you'll be behind schedule by 15,000 words.

## STEP 8: RUN AWAY FROM IT

Get up, put on your jogging shoes, and take off. Don, a failure analyst, says that after a mile or so of *not* thinking about the proposal, a flash of clarity enters his head and he has a solution to whatever he was stuck on. He picks up the pace, eager to get back to his computer.

When you are running away from your writing, be grateful you're in good company:

- Richard Feynman, the Nobel Prize winner who worked on the first atomic bomb and helped solve the mystery of the faulty O-rings that caused the *Challenger* disaster, got away from his writing by going to topless bars.
- Einstein distanced himself from his writing by going up to his study and reading Emily Post's book on etiquette. His family could hear his laughter resounding through the house. If they went upstairs to check, he would read them whatever section he considered outlandishly funny.

## MORE LITTLE STEPS

The whole point of using *zazen* to get the proposal written in spite of yourself is to focus on little easy steps instead of the whole proposal. Here are six more little steps for keeping yourself mindful of only what you are doing at the moment, not all the things you need to do.

- **Poke holes in the job.** Kids have a joke: "How do you eat an elephant?" The answer: "One bite at a time." Break up the job of writing a proposal into small pieces. Then break those pieces into even smaller pieces, such as the first draft of the first part of section one. Now set deadlines for each small piece. Each morning you can say, "All I need to focus on today is this little bite."

- **Think "first draft."** What you put on the page does not have to be (and will not be) perfect. You will revise it, your prereviewers will recommend changes, and you'll polish it again.

- **Put stuff you don't know in brackets.** If you're missing a fact or a number or a reference, *do not* stop writing to go look it up. Just put brackets around it and go right on writing. For example, "There are [0000] trees in Russia."

- **Tell the world!** Tell your friends and your family or your manager what you plan to write and by when. Now you are on record, and you will not want to disappoint them (especially your manager). Don't just tell them the final deadline; announce the deadlines you've set for each piece of the job.

- **Write with a partner.** You'll discipline each other, just as you and your friend shamed each other into keeping up that aerobics class. It's also less lonely.

- **Reward yourself at every turn.** When your proposal is accepted, you will certainly be rewarded. But that reward is too distant and abstract to keep you at the keyboard. Promise yourself a specific reward when you finish section two or write your thousand words or write for two hours straight. You'll go for a run or buy some Ben & Jerry's ice cream—not the low-fat stuff, but Cherry Garcia.

---

Liane Reif-Lehrer, a reviewer of grant applications for the National Institutes of Health and author of the *Grant Application Writer's Handbook*, recommends that you have a good second draft of your proposal ready for prereviewers ten weeks before the application is due.

---

Kevin, who is on a team that writes proposals for navigation devices, was delighted to find that when he puts something in brackets, such as [what's the model number on that GPS?], someone else on the team will actually fill in the information for him.

## ZAZEN AND NOT WRITING

When writers think about a whole proposal looming in front of them, they can get stuck. To free yourself, you need to find a state of tranquillity, as you do in meditation. Don't think, just breathe. Focus mindfully on little easy steps instead of the whole proposal. Respectfully want to write it, but don't allow yourself to consider the whole. Just be mindful of each step and each event. In this seemingly purposeless approach, you'll get the proposal written in spite of yourself.

# The Zen of Archery

**BREAKING THROUGH YOUR INTERNAL CENSORS**

*Try not. Do, or do not. There is no try.*

—YODA

Sometimes the most difficult part of writing a proposal is breaking through our internal censors—the inhibitions we have about whether what we say will be important or understood. We push so hard worrying about how our ideas will be accepted, we can't get started at all. Or we write in that formal, opaque style that puts the reader to sleep. Some of these barriers are just our natural fear of being laughed at, but some of them are set up by our professional training and by our very noble attempts to get organized. How can we recognize and work past these internal censors?

## RECOGNIZING THE INTERNAL CENSORS

We're all primed to write that proposal. We're going to just ready-aim-fire, but we get frozen at the keyboard. I've encountered three types of internal censors we face while writing. The most common is what I call "ready-aim-doubt"—that snide little voice that says, *This is terrible writing. Only an idiot would buy this. Do you expect to win the contract with* this *garbage?* In *Bird by Bird: Some Instructions on Writing and Life*, Anne Lamott says that her first draft would always be

> . . . so long and incoherent and hideous that for the rest of the day, I'd obsess about getting creamed by a car before I could write a

decent second draft. I'd worry that people would read what I'd written and believe that the accident had really been a suicide, that I had panicked because my talent was waning and my mind was shot.

The truth is, as Hemingway said, "All first drafts are shit." And no matter how much you fiddle with that first draft, it will be very bad.

Do not try to stifle this internal censor. Just agree with it for the time being. Just say to that voice in a kindly way, *Of course this is garbage, but it will smell better tomorrow.* As Bob Marley sang, "Everything gonna be awright." Say to yourself, *Not yet brilliant? Maybe not, but wait until I rewrite it tomorrow. It will be okay. Not great, but serviceable.*

Be courteous to this internal censor: you're going to need it later when you start revising.

The second type of internal censor is called "aim, aim, aim, then think very carefully about firing." In my Toastmasters club, we found that people from many exacting disciplines—scientists, engineers, business consultants, teachers—could give delightful, clear speeches about many subjects. But when they tried to give speeches about their own fields, the speeches were dry, dull, and hard to understand.

Professional training teaches us to get organized, set a precise goal, and home in on it. It teaches us to be orderly, methodical, deductive. Like carpenters, we are taught to "measure twice, cut once." But we can get so caught up in measuring, so fearful of making a mistake, that we never make the cut. We forget that we're going to have many chances to refine this draft, polish it, and correct our errors. But we won't have anything to refine, polish, or correct unless we get something down in the first place.

Some writers try to avoid this problem of being too methodical by making no plans at all. Their technique is the third type of internal censor, called "ready-fire-then aim later." They don't plan their writing; they don't make any kind of outline. But because they have been programmed from elementary school to aim, they

> Our thoughts and feelings flow like a river. If we try to stop the flow of a river, we will meet the resistance of the water. It is better to flow with it, and then we may be able to guide it in ways we want it to go. We must not attempt to halt it.
>
> —THICH NHAT HANH

end up trying to plan, organize, structure, and perfect the proposal while they are typing. This is the sure way to spend the next three months stuck on that perfect first sentence and never write the proposal.

The techniques of Zen archery can help us blast past all these internal censors.

## READY, READY, DON'T AIM, DON'T FIRE

Eugen Herrigal, a German teacher of philosophy, wrote a short, beautiful book called *Zen in the Art of Archery.* Herrigal was teaching philosophy at the University of Tokyo and wanted to learn about Zen. One way to understand Zen was to study Zen archery. Through a friend, he persuaded a Master of archery to train him. Herrigal assumed he would be good at archery because he'd been good at shooting a pistol on a firing range. He found it didn't help at all.

In Zen archery, he was not to even *think* about the target. For two years he was trained in how to hold the bow and how to breathe. Even after two years, when they actually used targets, it was not important whether the arrow hit the target. The important thing was to achieve a meditative repose, a state of relaxation and control of breathing that allowed the arrow to fly from the bow without any effort or even thought on his part.

It took Herrigal six years to master this philosophy—years you certainly don't have when trying to write a proposal. But some of the ideas in Zen archery can help us get words down on paper. I call it "direct writing." The idea—just as in Zen archery—is to take a concept directly from the inspiration to action with no interference from the intellect. It's a way to break through our internal censors so we can get our ideas down clearly and simply.

Direct writing bypasses the problems of ready-aim-doubt; aim, aim, aim, then think very carefully about firing; and ready-fire-then aim later—just by getting *ready.* Achieving an inner preparedness, an attitude of acceptance. You avoid thinking about the target or how you're going to hit it. You avoid thinking about the proposal or how you're going to write it. The steps are simple, but like the archer's training, they may take some time to learn:

Don't think: just breathe.
Get ready.

Don't aim.
Don't fire.

Let's take them one step at a time.

## Don't Think: Just Breathe

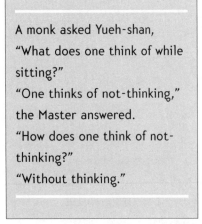

A monk asked Yueh-shan, "What does one think of while sitting?"
"One thinks of not-thinking," the Master answered.
"How does one think of not-thinking?"
"Without thinking."

In the 1950s, IBM issued desk signs to all its employees. The sign read, "THINK!" The motto for IBM Global Services is now "People who think. People who do. People who get it." Our motto for direct writing is "Don't Think. Just Do." (You can worry about getting it later.)

The first thing Herrigal had to learn in Zen archery was how to hold the bow in a relaxed mood, without straining and stiffening his arm and shoulder muscles. He found it impossible because pulling the bow apart required great strength. Months later the Master taught him how to breathe to relax his muscles, which he also found difficult. Once to excuse himself, he told the Master he was "conscientiously making an effort to keep relaxed." The Master replied, "That's just the trouble, you make an effort to think about it. Concentrate entirely on your breathing, as if you had nothing else to do!"

In direct writing, you concentrate entirely on your moving fingers, not where you must be going. Don't try to force the writing, and don't try to follow a rigid structure. Follow your outline in general, but don't think about the final version. Think: *Draft, first draft, first very rough draft.*

Forget entirely about format, spelling, and even grammar. Some word-processing programs now mark spelling and grammar errors on your screen while you type. Mine puts words it thinks are misspelled in red and underlines grammar problems in green. Very useful later. But not now.

For direct writing, change the format preferences on your word-processing program so it does *not* mark these errors while you type. You don't need some backseat-driver computer program leaning over your shoulder nagging you: *Made a mistake there, didn't you! Don't you think you should stop writing and fix it now?* If they persist in nagging you, darken your monitor.

Not thinking doesn't need to be rigid. You can choose to allow yourself to edit just a bit as you go if it feels better. We all nip our cursors up to fix trivial things: a typo, a misspelling. If you try to refrain from editing altogether, it will be like trying not to think at all while meditating. *Don't think. Just breathe. Omigod, that was a thought. Don't think don't think don't think. How can I not think? Don't think!*

No. What you do is let the thoughts drift in and out. You don't prevent yourself from thinking, but you let the thoughts drift away while you focus again on your breathing. Yes, edit little stuff if inspired to, then focus again on your writing.

## Get Ready

Herrigal talks about any creative artist getting ready by "summoning forth this presence of mind before all doing and creating, before ever he begins to devote himself to his work." Herrigal then describes the archer getting ready:

> The archer, kneeling to one side and beginning to concentrate, rises to his feet, ceremoniously steps up to the target and, with a deep obeisance, offers the bow and arrow like consecrated gifts, then nocks the arrow, raises the bow, draws it and waits in an attitude of supreme spiritual alertness.

You'd look pretty silly kneeling and bowing before your computer, but there are other ways to get into an attitude of repose:

- Some people listen to music.
- Some meditate.
- Others write in a journal.
- I build three-dimensional jigsaw puzzles.

In the Japanese art of *sumi* painting, the painter must also take time to get ready. *Sumi* ink comes in a solid block about three inches long. You first rub the block against the side of the stone wall of a small well containing water. Then you mix the abraded ink particles with the water slowly until you have the ink of the thickness or darkness you want. You fill the brush with just the right amount of ink. Herrigal describes a painter teaching a class. The painter carefully prepares his ink and brush, then

. . . straightens the long strip of paper that lies before him on the mat, and finally, after lapsing for a while into profound concentration, in which he sits like one inviolable, he produces with rapid, absolutely sure strokes, a picture which, capable of no further correction and needing none, serves the class as a model.

With *sumi* painting, no corrections are possible. Once that brush of black ink has swept across the paper, the painting is done. It cannot be changed. Thus the need to prepare yourself before painting. With writing on the computer, infinite corrections are not only possible, but trivially easy. Why not be bold?

> Spend ten years observing bamboo,
>
> become a bamboo yourself,
>
> then forget everything and—paint.
>
> —Old saying quoted by Herrigal

The ancient Babylonians wrote contracts by digging the words into wet clay tablets with a stick. After the contract was signed by both parties, another tablet was laid on top and they were sealed together. Then they wrote the contract again on the outside of the top tablet. If a dispute arose over the contract, they could always break open the two tablets to view the original sealed contract. Why did they have to go to this elaborate trouble? Because anyone could wet the clay again and change the words! If the Babylonians could make changes later, how much easier for you who have a delete key or at least an eraser.

Getting ready is a way to calm yourself to prepare for work, to achieve what Herrigal calls "that vital loosening" that will put you in a playful, creative frame of mind. In this "I don't care" repose, the words will burst forth before they can be censored. The aim is not to get slap-happy or achieve inertial tranquillity, but to find a state of purposeless tension. That's the Zen approach to writing: respectfully wanting to write it and not getting frustrated if it doesn't get written.

## Don't Aim

Get real, you're saying. If you don't aim, how can you expect to hit the target? If doing things linearly works for you, keep at it. If preparing a rigid outline, setting a schedule, and following that schedule come hell or high water works for you, stop reading here. But if you find yourself frustrated, if, like me, you find yourself snapping at co-workers because you aren't meeting that writing schedule, why not try another way?

Not aiming is hard because we are trained to aim. Here are three ways to reverse this training:

- Ignore the real target.
- Imagine the job is already done.
- Just play.

### Ignore the Real Target

Once we lived in a big old house in San Jose that had a wonderful large kitchen. The problem was, the large kitchen had a large, white-tiled floor, and our household included three children—one who delighted in dropping food off her high chair and watching it splat on the white floor. By the time I got around to cleaning the floor, it was far too dirty for a quick mop.

On weekends, after a full work week, I'd look at that huge filthy floor and think, *No way can I scrub that whole floor.* When I went into another room, the kitchen floor haunted me. Finally, I bargained with myself: *I'll just scrub four squares of tile.* I filled a pail with hot soapy water, got a big sponge, and sat on the floor. I scrubbed four tiles. Done! Now I could quit. But how beautiful those four clean tiles looked. While I was down on the floor, I decided to scrub just four more. The floor always got cleaned.

Ignore your long-term target. Forget getting the grant, winning the Nobel Prize, signing the book contract, making the sale, or banking the venture capitalist's millions. Then forget your short-term goals: your proposal deadline or the deadline for this section. Just write.

### Imagine the Job Is Already Done

A second way to train yourself not to aim is to do a time warp. I learned this idea in a workshop on how to avoid stress over deadlines, and it has become my surefire way to eliminate the energy wasted in worrying about time. Instead of fretting about getting the proposal written on time, imagine that it's already written. Imagine you have already received confirmation from the express courier that your client received the proposal on time. Get yourself firmly in that future time zone. It's done. It's over. Whew.

Now mentally go back and watch yourself do it. Notice the steps you took, the plans you made, the words you wrote. Take yourself slowly through the process of writing and revising and refining that proposal. See yourself handing the finished proposal package to the courier. Notice how well you did it, in great detail, step by step.

Now that you've seen the goal already achieved, forget the goal. Sit down and write as if you had no purpose. Just keep going. Keep your fingers moving. Don't stop to ponder the perfect word. To keep moving forward, I put a slash as a code after a word and then add the word I think is better/superior/clearer. Pretend you are transcribing a tape and the tape is moving forward and you must keep up.

Just Do It

—NIKE SLOGAN

For later inserts, type "blah, blah" as a place holder so you can put it aside in your mind. Sometimes I hit bold and enter **"boring, boring, boring"** right in the middle of the sentence. Know that you can always fix it later. If something troubles you, say, "Yeah, yeah, I'll take care of that." Write yourself a note—"[fix this stuff later]"—and keep on typing. My mother called it "giving it a lick and a promise."

### Just Play

Just playing isn't some new age fluffy idea. Many great ideas come when we decide to just play. Richard Feynman got the germ of the idea that won him the Nobel Prize when he decided he was just going to play with physics and not worry about any importance to it at all. Here's how he tells it:

I was in the cafeteria and some guy, fooling around, throws a plate in the air. As the plate went up in the air, I saw it wobble, and I noticed the red medallion of Cornell on the plate going around. It was pretty obvious to me that the medallion went around faster than the wobbling.

I had nothing to do, so I start to figure out the motion of the rotating plate. I discover that when the angle is very slight, the medallion rotates twice as fast as the wobble rate—two to one. It came out of a complicated equation! Then I thought, "Is there some way I can see in a more fundamental way, by looking at the forces or the dynamics, why it's two to one?" I ultimately worked out what the motion of the mass particles is, and how all the accelerations balance to make it come out two to one. I went on to work out equations of wobbles. Then I thought about how electron orbits start to move in relativity. . . .

It was effortless. It was easy to play with these things. It was like uncorking a bottle: everything flowed out effortlessly. I almost tried to resist it! There was no importance to what I was doing, but ultimately, there was. The diagrams and the whole business that I got the Nobel Prize for came from that piddling around with the wobbling plate.

One way to allow yourself to just play is to pretend the proposal is not important. In fact, you are just doing it for fun and no one is ever going to read it. Diana Gabaldon, author of several smashing historical romance time travel novels, began writing her first best-selling book, *The Outlander*, just to practice writing a novel. She never planned to show it to anyone, so she was free do whatever she wanted.

Erase from your mind the need to win this proposal and imagine it's just a practice exercise. Imagine you're going to write it and then throw it away. Pretend you're writing it just for fun.

## Don't Fire

If you are struggling to write an idea and it just won't come, does it help to keep forcing it? No. Back off, get your mind on something else. I once got myself writing again by spending four days at a bed-and-breakfast on the California coast without any laptop, paper, or pen. I refused to allow myself to write for four days. I walked along the cliffs and took long baths in lavender soap by candlelight. I had picked this little town because it offered nothing to do. You sat staring at the ocean. If someone asked you what you were doing, you said: "I'm watching for whales." After four days, I itched to write. I hungered for my computer.

When Herrigal was trying to learn to release the bowstring smoothly, without a jerk that made the arrow wobble, the Master said, "Don't think of what you have to do, don't consider how to carry it out! The shot will go smoothly only when it takes the archer himself by surprise."

How can you let yourself be surprised? Don't fire. Just let the firing happen, the way a child releases your hand to run toward a balloon. I once wrote half of a novel and got stuck when the main character absolutely refused to have the affair

> . . . like every beginner,
> I thought you could beat,
> pummel, and thrash an idea
> into existence. Under such
> treatment, of course, any
> decent idea folds up its paws,
> turns on its back, fixes its
> eyes on eternity, and dies.
>
> —RAY BRADBURY
> in *Zen in the Art of Writing*

with a CIA agent I had planned for her. The whole novel hinged on her having this affair, but she kept showing up to meet him at the wrong time or in the wrong city. I wrote my friend Gene, who used to write for *The New Yorker*, ranting: How was I supposed to write this novel if this stubborn woman kept refusing to follow my plot? Gene wrote back:

Who could ask for anything more? It means you've brought her alive. Let her go her own way, make the book be what she wants it to be. Anyway, solve it with your fingers, not your head.

Don't fire. Get yourself into a state of repose and purposeless tension, then let your fingers solve it. Getting in this state will allow you to get ideas down the instant your mind conceives them without any interference from your internal censors.

## TIPS FOR BREAKING THROUGH YOUR INTERNAL CENSORS

Practice direct writing as a way of taking a concept directly from the inspiration to action with no interference from your intellect. Remember that your professional training has programmed you to be objective, set a hypothesis, be orderly, methodical, deductive. Here's how to break those rules:

- Don't think: just breathe. Don't even try to relax.
- Get ready. Assume a state of purposeless tension by meditating or listening to music. Get into an "I don't care" repose where the words just burst forth.
- Don't aim. Ignore your real targets—first, the long-term target, then the short-term deadlines. Do the time warp, where you imagine the job is already done successfully. Just play.
- Don't fire. Don't struggle to write it right. Just let it come. Let yourself be surprised by what your fingers write.

# We Are All a Part of the Universe

## BUT WILL YOU WRITE BEST ALONE OR ON A TEAM?

The Zen concept of *kensho* is self-realization, seeing into yourself clearly. The *Tao-te Ching* says, "He who knows others is wise. He who knows himself is enlightened." Writing a proposal alone can be scary, but at least you make your own rules. Writing a proposal as part of a team presents different problems and different opportunities. To deal with these problems and take advantage of these opportunities, you need to understand your own nature.

Team writing requires coordinating with other people, compromising, and relinquishing control. If you hate all that, writing on a team will be frustrating. But writing on a team also offers support from others, real-time feedback, and confirmation of your ideas. That can be rewarding. Because you may not be given a choice about writing on a team, it helps to look ahead to see how you will react to it. You can do that by understanding

- how you prefer to work and learn.
- what you want or don't want from interacting with a group.
- how much control you need or are willing to relinquish.

By understanding your needs, you will be better equipped to either take advantage of the rewards of working on a team or learn how to stay serene in a potentially frustrating style of working.

How will you feel about writing on a team? Here's a pop quiz. It's not ordered or scientific, and it's transparent and easy to score. Don't take it too seriously, just relax and circle your favorite answer to each question.

## THE TEAM QUIZ

1.  If you put a doormat in front of your door, what would it say?
    a.  Party on Down!
    b.  Welcome
    c.  Wipe Your Feet
    d.  Go Away
2.  Which game would you prefer to play and with whom?
    a.  Play charades at a party with friends
    b.  Play touch football with the Kennedys
    c.  Play racquetball with business rivals
    d.  Play chess by mail with strangers
3.  If you were to play roulette, how would you play it?
    a.  I'd play roulette in formal dress at Monte Carlo
    b.  I'd play roulette at a charity fund-raiser
    c.  I'd be the croupier at Monte Carlo
    d.  I'd play Russian roulette
4.  If you were to join an on-line chat group, what would you do?
    a.  Become the host
    b.  Interact when I have something to say
    c.  Monitor other users
    d.  Lurk on line
5.  If you had to choose one of these for a vacation, which would you choose?
    a.  High school reunion at Disneyland
    b.  Club Med in the Bahamas
    c.  Outward Bound in the Sierras
    d.  Silent retreat in Nepal
6.  How did you do your homework in high school?
    a.  I went to a friend's house.
    b.  I kept the radio playing in my room for company.
    c.  I organized a study group.
    d.  I studied in a secret carrel at the library.

7. How do you get an important message to someone?
   a. I go see them in person.
   b. I talk to them on the phone.
   c. I send e-mail.
   d. I send express voice mail to avoid talking.

8. When you go to a party, how do you get there?
   a. I call around until I'm sure I can share a ride with someone (my car or theirs).
   b. I ride with a friend if it's convenient for both of us.
   c. I always take my car so I can leave when I feel like it.
   d. I don't go.

9. How do you travel on vacation?
   a. I always go on a group tour, in fact, the same group for the last ten years.
   b. I usually travel with friends or family.
   c. If I travel with others, I set a strict schedule for them.
   d. I set off alone, even to Romania.

10. How do you feel when someone orders for you in a restaurant?
    a. I feel cherished.
    b. It's okay. Maybe I'll get to try something new.
    c. I hate it.
    d. I get up and walk out.

11. Which of these statements bothers you most?
    a. Why do we need to go *together*?
    b. I dunno, Marty, whadda *you* wanna do?
    c. You can't *not* go!
    d. But I can't go *alone*.

12. How would you describe your desk at *work*?
    a. I keep it neat and clean most the time.
    b. Hopeless. I'm always trying to clear it off.
    c. I don't mind it messy, because I can always find what I want.
    d. I work on the floor.

*(continued on page 96)*

THE TEAM QUIZ *(continued)*

13. What is your style for working at *home?*
    a. I work best while eating in bed in front of the TV.
    b. I work best after everyone in the house or neighborhood is asleep.
    c. I work best in a neighborhood café.
    d. I work best at four A.M. in a dark warehouse.

14. Have you ever fantasized about
    a. spending the night with Brad Pitt or Britney Spears? (For older quiz takers, Paul Newman or Marilyn Monroe?)
    b. receiving a Nobel or Pulitzer Prize?
    c. Being Alan Greenspan?
    d. finally getting some peace and quiet by being sent to solitary confinement?

15. On airplanes, which do you hope for most?
    a. I'll make a lifelong friend of the stranger in the next seat.
    b. I'll have an empty seat next to me.
    c. I'll get to land the plane.
    d. I'll succeed in pretending I can't speak English to avoid talking to my seatmate.

16. What's the first *important* thing you do on an airplane?
    a. Buy my seatmate a drink.
    b. Watch the flight attendants do the emergency drill pantomime.
    c. Check the ETA and the pilot's credentials.
    d. Pull out my laptop.

17. What is your attitude about writing? Choose one.
    a. The best part of writing is the feeling of reaching out to everyone in the universe.
    b. The worst part of writing is being alone.
    c. The best part of writing is I get to choose life or death for my characters.
    d. The best part of writing is being alone.

18.  When there's a crucial playoff game, what do you do?
    a.  I invite all my friends over for a party.
    b.  I watch at home with a friend.
    c.  I go to the stadium/arena/field/ice rink/dog track/chicken house because I need to be there!
    d.  I read about it in the papers the next day.

19.  How do you feel about people coming over to your house?
    a.  I actually talk to Jehovah Witnesses.
    b.  I like it when friends just drop in.
    c.  I don't open the door unless people call first.
    d.  I never open the door.

20.  When you were in school, which did you do?
    a.  Join a sorority or fraternity and actually live in the house?
    b.  Join a sorority or fraternity or feel disappointed because you weren't asked to join?
    c.  Turn down a sorority or fraternity bid?
    d.  Refuse to even rush?

21.  What is your attitude about roommates?
    a.  I still see my roommates after all these years.
    b.  I never had a roommate I could abide for more than six months.
    c.  I require a roommate to submit references and sign a contract.
    d.  I never had or wanted to have a roommate.

22.  How do you feel about people who are cheerful and noisy in the morning?
    a.  I leap up and sing "Good Morning, Starshine" with them.
    b.  I ask them to wait until after I've had my coffee.
    c.  A cheerful roommate automatically breaks our written contract.
    d.  I've killed people for less.

23.  If you didn't have to worry about clothes for warmth or social reasons, how would you dress for work?
    a.  I'd wear a taffeta ball gown or a NASA space suit.
    b.  I'd wear jeans and a T-shirt.
    c.  I'd wear whatever I felt like wearing.
    d.  I'd work naked at my terminal.

*(continued on page 98)*

THE TEAM QUIZ *(concluded)*

24.–30. In your next life, what do you want to do for a living? (Across each row, choose *only one* from each column.)

| COLUMN A | COLUMN B | COLUMN C | COLUMN D |
|---|---|---|---|
| Zoo Keeper | Housekeeper | Babysitter with Light Housekeeping | Lighthouse Keeper |
| Head Waiter | Headhunter (in business) | Head *Hunter* (on safari) | *Head* Hunter (in jungle) |
| Cab Driver | Limousine Driver | Mule Team Driver | Long-Distance Truck Driver |
| Literary Agent | Writer | Book Editor | Ghost Writer |
| Gossip Columnist | Newspaper Reporter | TV Anchor | Obituary Writer |
| On-Line Chat Group Host | Computer Programmer | Bill Gates | Hacker |
| Tupperware Salesperson | Jolly Green Giant | Mr. Clean | Maytag Repairman |

## How to Score and Interpret the Quiz

First, count up how many questions you answered in each category. Give yourself 5 points for each "a" answer, 4 points for each "b" answer, 3 points for each "c" answer, and 2 points for each "d" answer. Total your scores and find the range where you fit below to predict how well you'd work on a team.

| ANSWER | POINTS | SCORES |
|---|---|---|
| Total "a" answers = | Times 5 points | = |
| Total "b" answers = | Times 4 points | = |
| Total "c" answers = | Times 3 points | = |
| Total "d" answers = | Times 2 points | = |
| Total Score | | = |

## Score Range

121–150    You are an exceedingly outgoing, sociable person who is more comfortable when someone else takes the lead. Writing on a team will be fun for you, and you could be a great contributor. You would probably be lonely and frustrated trying to write by yourself.

91–120    You are comfortable interacting with a group or going it alone. Allowing others to lead doesn't bother you too much, so you can work well on a team. Writing on a team will help you keep moving forward and give you confidence.

71–90    You have a strong need for control. You will be frustrated writing on a team unless you are the team leader. If you cannot lead the team, you'll need to find ways to control your parts of the proposal or manage other aspects such as the scheduling.

60–70    You are a determined loner who doesn't need or want to interact with a group. Writing on a team will be agony for you. Go off and write your assigned section and turn it in early so you can get back to your own writing. Or join a Zen monastery.

## WHAT IT'S LIKE WRITING ON A TEAM

Two writers, desperate to finish their screenplay, seclude themselves in a seedy hotel room, ordering room service and refusing to let the maids come in to clean. Harry sits at the portable typewriter, a cigarette hanging from his lips, two fingers poised over the keys. Ralph roves the room, waving his arms. He stops, puts his fingers to his mouth, and says, "I've got it! The fugitive shouts, 'You'll never take me alive!' and leaps over the cliff."

Harry gives him a look of weary disdain.

"Guess not," says Ralph.

Then Harry starts typing madly, two fingers pounding over the keys.

"What is it?" asks Ralph, running to peer over Harry's shoulder. "That's it, that's it!" he shouts as Harry pounds away.

*Only in the movies.* When I see a book by two authors, I figure one has spent the time sitting

> *Getting together with a partner to write a book is like getting three people together to have a baby.*
>
> —Anonymous

and talking while the other took notes, then ran home and typed up the notes into a section of the book.

Writing on a corporate proposal team usually goes like this. The proposal leader works up an outline and assigns sections to various writers. The writers go off and write their sections, then the proposal leader puts them all together. The whole proposal is then copied or routed on-line for review by all the writers.

At this point, everyone has a chance to hack away at the others' writing. Editing other people's writing can be a lot of fun. There is no stronger urge than to revise someone else's draft. This pleasure can be reversed, however, when you find that *your* writing has been changed. Try to be calm about this.

How can you stay serene when someone is tampering with your gorgeous section? Alternative one is to try considering it a blessing that you don't have to write the whole proposal by yourself. If you scored below 90 points on the quiz, this will not work for you.

Alternative two is to use the concession theory suggested in a booklet from the Environmental Protection Agency: If a sentence was not clear to the other proposal writers, it's probably not going to be clear to the client. Do you want to change it now while you still have *some* control of the proposal, or do you want to let the clients try to "clarify" it to meet their own preconceptions? The EPA booklet says:

> Realizing that there are always other ways to get the point across will help you avoid "I'm right, you're wrong" confrontations. Using the concession theory, you can say, "Let's change it to make the point clearer."

Remember, the goal is not to preserve *your* style, but to smooth many writing styles into one uniform, coherent whole. Remaining calm is more difficult, of course, if your section is deleted or put into an appendix.

When the proposal team has agreed on a pretty solid draft, the managers get a chance to review it. A few managers will read the whole proposal; most will read only the executive summary and the contractual/cost section. If you're lucky, they will spot glaring omissions and confusing statements in your summary. This is lucky? Yes. Who would you rather find these errors—your manager or your client? Your manager may make sweeping changes or make your team rewrite the whole summary. This is also good; it will make your proposal stronger. (If you're as lucky as I was, the editor of your book will do the same.)

At some point, you and the other writers lose all control over the words you have written as the proposal leader and the editor discuss further changes. This may actually be a relief to you. If it bothers you, just let it go. Think about next time, when you'll be the proposal leader.

## AVOIDING CHAOS TO ACHIEVE SERENITY

Even if you're the leader of the proposal team, you won't have *total* control of when and how things come together at the end. You have to trust that everyone will get his or her piece done right and at the right time. Some will, and some won't. How can you win this proposal without increasing your medication?

- At the outset, give all the writers a detailed outline of the whole proposal with page limits for each section as well as a clear schedule for getting the sections written.
- Make it very clear that once the writers have given you their sections, they *cannot* make changes to the version on their own computers. Assure them they will be given the chance to make as many changes as they want, but *only* on your one master copy.
- Realize that many writers will not grasp this concept and will keep sending you revised versions of their sections. Emphasize that you will ignore these new versions.
- Assume that Harry's section will be late and Harriet's will be much too long.
- Schedule time for thoroughly rewriting the executive summary after your manager reads it.
- Know that no matter how carefully you plan, something *will* go wrong. Just hope it is something small or it occurs early in the game. Someone showed that 90 percent of the effort on a proposal is put forth in the last 10 percent of the time schedule. If a disaster occurs during that last 10 percent of the schedule, you won't have time to recover from it. So make your big push on the proposal early in the schedule, not at the end.
- Assume some emergency will occur: power blackout, earthquake, tornado, or hurricane. Think about the worst thing that could happen. Then make contingency plans: How will you get the proposal done if an emergency occurs?
- Be serene, knowing you are prepared.

# THREE THINGS YOU SHOULD *NOT* DO AS TEAM LEADER

If you are the line manager of the team writing the proposal, you already have control. Here you need to be careful, because this isn't the only proposal you want this team to write. You need to look ahead to the day they'll do it on their own.

Good managers want the people they supervise to learn independence, so they make the mistake of telling a new person: "Here's your chance to learn how to write a proposal. You take charge of this proposal. Go write it on your own, and when you're done, bring it to me and I'll look it over." Sounds as though the manager is empowering the person, doesn't it? Yes, but he's also terrifying her. The scary words are "when you're done." The new proposal writer will go off and kill herself trying to write a perfect, finished proposal. She will work late trying *to be done.* Then she brings it to the manager, and of course he says, "No, this isn't quite what I had in mind." Arrghhhhhhhhhh.

Here are three things to avoid as a manager of people who need to write proposals.

## Don't Expect Someone You Manage to Read Your Mind

First, sit down with the new writer and talk about the proposal. Discuss the approach you think will work; let him or her suggest changes. Don't stop working together until you agree on the strategy for winning this proposal. Assign the proposal in stages: "First, give me your ideas for an outline. Then, let's look at this outline together."

## Don't Rewrite Their Stuff

The most common complaint in my writing workshops is: "No matter what I do, my boss always changes what I write." People who start out eager to learn to write well give up "because my boss going to rewrite it anyway." If you want your subordinates to learn to write well, don't rewrite their stuff. Don't rewrite even a few sentences. Resist changing even just a word here and there.

George, the manager of a successful group of engineers, demanded that the people in his group become good writers. But he *never* changed people's words.

I just make a light pencil mark in the margin. Not a check mark or an "X" like teachers use. That's means *wrong*. Just a light neutral mark. Then I go talk to the writers. At each pencil mark, I tell them where I was unsure what was meant. Or I make suggestions for making it clearer. But I never make the changes myself. If I redo it, they will never learn. If they know they're going to have to keep rewriting it themselves until it's clear, they'll learn sooner.

## Don't Insist on Your Style

Sometimes, no matter how good the writing is, the manager changes it: "Just needed to put it in our style." Well, "our style" is really the manager's style. Of course, the manager wants the writing to be clear, simple, and directed to the client. But that can done in many ways. As long as the writing is clear and useful, don't insist it be exactly like your way of writing. If that's what you wanted, you could just as well have written it yourself.

# WE ARE ALL PART OF THE UNIVERSE

How comfortably you work on a team depends on how well you understand your own needs and the needs of others on the team. Yasutani Roshi said, "The fundamental delusion of humanity is to suppose that I am here and you are out there." Whether you are leader of the proposal team or one of its members ultimately doesn't matter. You are simultaneously part of the group and an individual out there alone. In neither position will you have absolute control. In either position, you can successfully steer the proposal away from chaos and toward serenity.

# Worldwide Zen

## 11

## THE PROPOSAL THAT'S GOING OVERSEAS

So far in this book, we've been looking at the task of writing proposals to readers who share our culture and our language. We've seen problems enough in learning to write so clearly that the client cannot possibly misunderstand our ideas. Sending a proposal to international clients who have different cultures and languages adds layers of complexity and a high potential for misunderstanding. First, let me give you some simple some guidelines for ensuring that your proposal doesn't get lost in translation. Then, let me tell you a story about how it really goes.

## BE KEENLY AWARE OF GEOGRAPHICAL AND CULTURAL DIFFERENCES

Don't say you will visit your client "next summer" if your proposal is going south of the equator. You'll want to visit your Australian clients in *our* winter (December) while they are enjoying the beach.

If your proposal is going to a country like Zambia, where phone systems often break down, don't ask for an immediate reply by fax.

When you send a proposal to Japan, do not expect a fast acceptance. There must first be a long consensus process, followed by a flurry of questions you must respond to immediately. When your Japanese client says yes, it does not mean you have won the contract. It means they have received your proposal and are presenting it to their managers. Similarly, because of the Japanese culture of politeness, they will never say no outright. When they say, "There may be a slight complication in funding this proposal," it means they are certainly going to turn you down. If they say, "It may be difficult to fund this," it means they wouldn't fund your proposal unless they were desperate and it was the only proposal they received.

Look at the tone of your writing to see if it matches the tone of that culture. Our direct, breezy American prose may seem rude to a company in South America, where people still end their business letters with phrases such as "As always, we remain, Your obedient servants." If you face a choice between informal and formal writing, go with formal.

If you're sending a proposal to England, decide whether you're going to use American spelling (color, behavior, analyze, defense) or British spelling (colour, behaviour, analyse, defence). Then stick to it.

## CONSIDER YOUR INTERNATIONAL CLIENT'S PERSPECTIVE

If your proposal is going to an international client, you need to put yourself into that client's perspective. Consider carefully what words like these will mean to your client:

domestic/foreign
imports/exports
Eastern/Western

And where *is* "overseas"?

Make sure your executive summary covers all the important points in the proposal, because it may be the only section translated for the top executive. The big guys can read English, but they like the luxury of reading in their own language.

If your whole proposal is going to be translated, be sure to allow enough time for the translator to do a good job without staying up all night. Also allow time for someone on your team who speaks that language to read the translated version. You want to have *some* idea what your client is actually reading.

Words mistranslated can drastically change your meaning. A Chinese client once asked us to evaluate a new product. Our report told them the plastic device worked fine. But we also told them, "Customer acceptance could be affected by the device's ethereal odor." What we meant was, the device stank of ether. But when "ethereal" was translated as "celestial," the client couldn't understand why we were proposing additional funds to study odor masking.

Avoid expressions that are just clichés in English but may become very strange when translated:

quantum leap
low profile
covers the whole spectrum

Watch out for phrases that will be misleading in translation:

opens the door to
sheds light on
starting from scratch
synthetic chemist
fast lane

Jargon that is clear within a field such as business economics can become ludicrous in another language or culture:

windfall or bluebird
bottom line
rainmaker
fast turnover

## UNINTENTIONAL PUNS FOUND IN PROPOSALS

In the next decade, an increase of about 20 percent is expected in the number of hospital beds as a result of faster patient turnover.

We have noticed a deep-seated trend toward not wearing girdles.

Hearing aids are hardly ever heard of in Taiwan.

The previous guidelines are practical advice for avoiding intercultural misunderstandings, and they make it sound easy. If only cultural and language differences were as easy to resolve as it seems on paper. Here's a true story about a proposal I worked on for the Japanese government.

## INTERNATIONAL PROPOSAL WRITING IN THE REAL WORLD

On my desk is the ultimate challenge of my career as a technical editor: a Request for Proposals from the government of Japan. Now it will all come together. My years of editing proposals in response to requests from the U.S. government and my years of studying the arts and philosophy of Japan. In the seventies, I studied *The Zen Book of Tea* and read Kenneth Rexroth's haiku translations. In the eighties, I read *Theory Z* to learn of the Japanese ways of doing business through consensus. Five years ago, I studied the Japanese language. Even today, I can go up to anyone Japanese and say, "How do you do. This is a book. My desk is red."

Now I am to apply all this experience to understanding this Japanese RFP. What a serene change it will be from the RFPs we receive from U.S. agencies, which are written by a committee of people who wake in the middle of the night to scribble instructions on torn scraps of paper napkins, which they carry into work to be typed directly into the instructions—never again read by any member of the committee.

I stroll placidly up the hall to our proposal coordinator, Sally.

"An RFP from Japan," I say, holding it out to her in both hands like an offering. "Look how slim it is!"

"Do they want it stapled or bound?"

Sally has correlated our hit rate on proposals over the past five years with her ability to ferret out that *one* sentence hidden in Section L.4.2.3.1.5a of a three-inch-thick RFP, requiring that the proposal be stapled *only* in the top left-hand corner or *not* stapled at all but held together with metal fasteners.

She has expanded this correlation into a theory all of us now believe: Government proposals are first screened by former employees of the Department of Motor Vehicles, sequestered in a windowless room until they eliminate their quota of proposals. They sit at a circle of tables surrounding a Dumpster. Each table is equipped with the type of bell that usually says "Ring for Service." As they find a reason to reject each proposal, they hit their bells, shout out the reason for rejection, and throw the proposal into the Dumpster.

*Bing.* "Volume four exceeds page limit by half a page!" Toss.
*Bing.* "Cover not typed in nonproportional ten-point Courier font!" Toss.
*Bing.* "Margins less than 2.54 centimeters!" Toss.

The bings come faster and faster as the reviewers become excited by community zeal and by the need to pee.

"Or do they want it in a three-ring binder?" says Sally.

"They want it on A4 international-size paper."

"Really?" she says, her eyes sparkling. "This is a new concept."

"And in Japanese."

"Talk to Brian. He's the expert on languages."

Brian has been editing for scientists and engineers so long, he has learned not only to read their language, but to speak it. He is the only person I know who willingly pronounces "prioritization."

"Brian, listen. We are bidding on a Japanese RFP."

"It is to be noted that this will not be a matter of a trivial nature," he says. "Prior to drafting of the proposal, reading of the instructions should be accomplished."

It is precisely here that my serenity starts to waver. I have one version of the RFP in Japanese and one version translated by our Tokyo office. The requirements are just as exacting as a U.S. government RFP. And just as clear.

Brian and I now visit one of our proposal authors, who is Japanese. "Please look at the Japanese version and tell us what it means here, where it says: 'Close R&D Initial of Listing.'"

"Yes, yes," he says, smiling.

"Do they mean close or close? I mean, is it an adjective or a verb?"

"Yes, yes. Verb."

"Is there a verb in the Japanese version?"

"Yes. Verb is *is.*"

"Verb is is?"

"Yes."

"It would seem to be apparent that viable elucidation is not to be forthcoming," says Brian.

"But Brian, he says the verb is *is!*"

"I got that much," says Brian, lapsing into the vernacular.

"No, listen. The Japanese verb contained in this instruction is equivalent to one form of the English infinitive *to be.*"

Brian stares sightless at the computer's screen saver for several minutes, then says slowly, "Of course. Tabulation of experience closely relevant to this proposal is to be accomplished initially."

We have it now: List your most relevant experience at the beginning of the proposal.

We go on to the next instruction.

I write a summary of the RFP and make an outline of the proposal for the six proposal authors. "But it's all backward," they say. "How can we give our final goal first, the background in the middle, and only at the end describe what we will do in the first year?"

"Let me get back to you."

Brian, Sally, and I consult with Gloria Mundy, who has learned peace through meditation and edits now solely by intuition.

"Here's what I have, Gloria. I am going to be editing a proposal, on an RFP written by the Japanese government and then translated into a certain form of English, to be written by six authors, who have nearly all learned English as a second language."

"Tell me about them," says Gloria as she lays out her tarot cards.

"The chemist is from Israel, the testing engineer is from Germany, the physicist is from India, the surface analyst is from Japan, the materials scientist is from Australia, and the computer modeling expert is from Mississippi."

"What is the date of the RFP?"

Gloria looks over her cards, throws the *I Ching,* and draws the astrological chart of the RFP. "You have been approaching this thing too linearly," she says, running her hands over the tarot cards. "We must shift to our right brains. We must approach this—"

"Spatially!" I say.

"A potentially viable alternative," says Brian.

"It could work," says Sally. "We could have the authors write the proposal starting at the end and writing toward the beginning. Then you just reverse it."

"And look," I say. "In English we read from left to right and from the top of the page to the bottom. But in Japan they start in the upper right-hand corner and read down the page, working their way down the columns from right to left."

"Hebrew also goes from right to left," says Sally. "All consonants, uninterrupted by any vowels."

"And Japanese has no articles, no future tense, and no difference between singular and plural verbs," I say.

"Negative. Spatial orientation has apparently been abandoned now."

"Right, Brian," says Sally. "Anyway, German has its verbs at the end of the sentence. All you have to do is loft them forward."

"And when the materials scientist learned to write in Australia, she was doing it upside down. Again, I just flip it. I wonder how they write in Hindi or Urdu?"

"In mystic circles," says Gloria.

"That leaves the computer expert from Mississippi," I say, "who writes about linearized muffin-tin orbitals."

"Which is, by its intrinsic nature, a spatial conceptualization."

After the proposal is written, I begin to untangle and reweave it spatially, thinking always how it may be translated into Japanese. What remains of my Zen calm is gradually replaced with Baptist resolve. I work straight through the weekend so I can begin sending sections to the translator in northern Japan. I learn to calculate the time difference between California and Japan with no effort.

On Sunday afternoon at three o'clock, as I e-mail the final sections, I think of the translator on the train, now going to work on Monday morning. I awaken in the night, having dreamed of muffin tins circling the earth, and imagine the translator spatially around the globe, carefully choosing from the three Japanese writing systems to craft our clear, brilliant prose into the subtleties and nuances of Japanese.

Two days before the proposal is due to the Japanese government, we receive the Japanese version.

"I wonder what it actually says," muses Sally.

Upstairs in the Japanese author's office, he frowns. "Yes, yes," he says. "This is very bad. I think they have used a machine to translate it."

"Machine?"

"Using computer to translate is very common in Japan."

"Give me an example."

"Well, here where we say, 'We will tailor the properties of the ceramic,' they have used the old Chinese character that means a tailor."

"You mean a person sitting cross-legged, snipping and sewing?"

"Yes, yes," he says.

We now enter phase two—daily questions from Japan and requests for more information. Sally calls it "death by a thousand faxes."

Our work is just beginning.

## WORLDWIDE ZEN

When your proposal is going to another country, you need to be aware of the cultural and geographical differences between you and your client. A difference in language is only one of the barriers—and it's a tough one. Other barriers can mean the difference between a proposal that wins and one that simply confuses your client. Put yourself keenly into the mental perspective of your client to overcome these barriers.

# PART THREE

# ZAZEN
# AGAIN

## Refine Your Proposal

# *Shibui*

## 12

## USING UNDERSTATED ELEGANCE TO GRACE YOUR STYLE

●

*A Zen Master acquired property with a beautiful view of the sea and planned to build a teahouse there. His students imagined sitting on the deck and drinking tea with that sweeping view of the ocean. But when the teahouse was finished and they arrived for the first tea ceremony, they found that a grove of trees had been planted between the teahouse and the ocean.*

*Honoring custom, they stopped at the pond to purify their hands and mouths before entering the teahouse. When they knelt to dip the water, they saw that an opening had been cut in the trees that framed a small, perfect view of the sea. As they poured water over their hands, they could connect the coolness of the water with the coolness of the sea.*

●

*Shibui* is a Japanese concept of beauty that is similar to the idea of "less is more." For example, the room for holding a tea ceremony is designed with clean lines and subdued colors, perhaps all in monochrome, varied only by different surfaces and textures. Within this spare simplicity will be one very small area of richness, such as one glowing purple iris.

If you work to make your writing clean and spare, your readers will find it easy to understand your ideas. And when you *do* have something dramatic to say, it will stand out and be remembered.

I got a lesson in *shibui* from my ten-year-old granddaughter when we spent an afternoon watching a pond of wild ducks. She asked me, "Do you know how to tell the males from the females?"

"Yes," I said. "The males are the pretty ones." The male ducks with their silvery feathers had striking blue-and-white tail feathers. Above their white necklaces, their heads glowed in deep amethyst that shifted to emerald as they moved through the light. The female ducks were a dowdy brown and white.

"The females *look* very plain," she said. "But they have a secret."

"What secret?"

"Pick one female duck and watch her closely."

I watched. When the female duck rose to walk toward the water, she lifted her wings briefly and I saw it: a tapering band of rich purple, banded in black and white, hiding under her wing feathers.

That's *shibui.*

The opposite of *shibui* is to relate everything in great agonizing detail without highlighting the important information. Repeat yourself a lot. Don't group information in a way that helps the reader absorb and remember it, just go on and on and on.

I once edited for a scientist who wrote very long reports. We're talking three inches thick, every one of them, no matter how long or short the project. His reports always sent me nodding away at my desk. The science was good. The work was thorough. But why were the reports so long and boring? He wrote just as he spoke—in a monotone. Everything was given equal weight. He never said, "As I described in detail in section two . . ." No, he explained it all again and always at the same level of detail. Nothing was highlighted. Nothing was interpreted. Just fact after fact after fact.

It reminded me of the way some people talk—the people you try to get away from fast. They say:

> You gotta hear this exciting thing that happened to me! I was getting ready to fly to L.A. last Tuesday—wait, was it Tuesday or Wednesday? No it was Wednesday, because I had the car serviced on Tuesday. Needed a tune-up real bad. Yeah, I think it *was* Wednesday. Yes, Wednesday. Because on Tuesday, I know I got home late after paying an enormous amount for that tune-up. God, what they charge nowadays. Anyway, I was planning to fly to L.A. and—have you booked a flight down there lately?

If you are forced to hang around long enough to actually hear the exciting thing that happened to this person, you will no longer care.

To hold your reader's attention, keep it brief, make it spare. Pare it down to the essentials needed to sell your idea. How do you do that? How do you use the idea of *shibui* to grace your style? Here are six ways I've found:

- Omit needless words.
- Avoid fad redundancies.
- Keep to the essentials.
- Avoid fancy words.
- Resist using technical words from another field.
- Quit trying to impress your reader.

## OMIT NEEDLESS WORDS

One simple way to get rid of the clutter is to omit needless words. Let me quote from Strunk and White's *The Elements of Style:*

> Vigorous writing is concise. A sentence should contain no unnecessary words, a paragraph no unnecessary sentences, for the same reason that a drawing should have no unnecessary lines and a machine no unnecessary parts. This requires not that the writer make all his sentences short, or that he avoid all detail and treat his subjects only in outline, but that every word tell.

Read it again, especially that last sentence. Our objective is to make "every word tell."

*The Elements of Style* is an example of *shibui* in itself. The original book written by Professor William Strunk Jr. at Cornell in 1918 was forty-three pages long and cost twenty-five cents. Strunk himself called it "the little book." He exhorted students, "Get the little book. Get the little book." When *The Elements of Style* was republished in 1959 with a new section on style written by one of Strunk's students, E. B. White of *The New Yorker,* it spent thirty-four weeks on *The New York Times* best-seller list. In the introduction, E. B. White remembers Strunk teaching these principles at Cornell:

> In the days when I was sitting in his class, he omitted so many needless words, and omitted them so forcibly and with such eagerness and obvious relish,

that he often seemed in the position of having shortchanged himself—a man left with nothing more to say yet with time to fill, a radio prophet who had outdistanced the clock. Will Strunk got out of this predicament by a simple trick: he uttered every sentence three times. When he delivered his oration on brevity to the class, he leaned forward over his desk, grasped his coat lapels in his hands, and, in a husky, conspiratorial voice, said, "Rule Seventeen. Omit needless words! Omit needless words! Omit needless words!"

How do you know which words are "needless"? Let's look at a sentence we've all seen many times:

In the event that you have any questions on this matter, please do not hesitate to contact the undersigned.

We won't lose any meaning whatsoever if we cut this sentence from nineteen words to eight:

If you have any questions, please contact me.

The sentence is also less stuffy. Let's try another:

During the course of the experiment, we made two different attempts to separate the by-products, but it became very clear that the quite hot mixture was turning red in color due to the fact that the beaker was in excessively close proximity to the heating element.

All those extra words are cluttering up the landscape. When we clear away the needless words and redundant expressions, we have this simpler sentence:

During the experiment, we made two attempts to separate the products, but the mixtures turned red because the beaker was too close to the heating element.

We've taken out words that have no added meaning:

the course of
different
due to the fact that

And we've pruned expressions that are redundant in themselves:

> very clear
> quite hot
> red in color
> in excessively close proximity

We've cut thirteen words and added only one, so we've saved twelve words.

My sister Barbara's motto for cleaning out the refrigerator applies just as well to writing: "If in doubt, throw it out." Omitting needless words will not only make your writing tighter, it's fun to do.

> A sign in the lobby of a hotel in San Diego:
>
> *For your information, additional elevators are around the corner.*

## AVOID FAD REDUNDANCIES

Some phrases are insidious because people have heard them so often, they believe the phrases are needed:

> current status
> in close proximity
> potential candidate
> completely destroyed
> lifelong native

Such words do not need modifying. *Status* already *means* the current situation, *proximity means* nearby, and *candidate* already contains the idea of potential. Phrases like *completely destroyed* and *lifelong native* become meaningless with an added adjective. No one can be slightly pregnant or almost clean.

Redundant phrases seem to creep into our language, become very popular, hang around a while, then saunter away, pretending to be indifferent when no one uses them anymore. *Viable alternative* has faded away along with the eighties. Very few people now use *hopefully*. People are abandoning the ubiquitous, unnecessary, annoying use of *basically*, as in this example:

I think that people are really realizing that basically, to put it bluntly, the lawyers are screwing them. They're charging phenomenal prices for things that basically the lawyers don't even do. Their secretaries do it. Law is not this mystical thing. Basically, people can do it themselves.

*Basically* has been used to mean everything from "essentially" to "fundamentally" to "in brief" to "Gee, I don't know what I'm going to say, so I'll pause here for a second." Let it wander away.

I've noticed a new fad poking its nose into news reports: *different*. I hear, "The police arrested two different suspects." As opposed to two same suspects? I read: "We tried two different methods of unlocking the door." "We spotted two different brands of toothpaste." Can there be two same methods, two same brands?

Found in a computer manual:

*The Merge Fields feature can be repeated infinitely many times.*

Another fad redundancy I hope will go away is *the reason why*. "The reason I want you to shut up" conveys all we need to know without adding *why*.

## DON'T DELETE THE ESSENTIALS

Omitting needless words and fad redundancies is so much fun—especially on someone else's writing—you can get carried away. We do not want "See Dick run" or "Me Tarzan, you Jane." Go back and read Strunk's Rule Seventeen again: "This requires not that the writer make all his sentences short, or that he avoid all detail and treat his subjects only in outline, but that every word tell." Here's what can happen when we cut the essentials.

The plastic bag warning "Keep out of the reach of children" always makes me want to say, "I try, but they're gaining on me." A more precise warning would be "Keep *this product* out of the reach of children."

I pondered with fascination the following sentence in a chemistry proposal:

Stir until the mixture does not dissolve.

Let's see, I'm stirring and it's dissolving and it's still dissolving. When will it stop dissolving? Sounds like a Zen idea for meditation. I asked the author,

"How can I stir until it does *not* dissolve?" What she meant was: "Keep adding the compound and stirring until you've added so much of the compound that the mixture will no longer dissolve." Oh.

Try explaining this one:

People do not use ballpoint pens until they run out of ink.

Does that mean a person waits until he or she runs out of ink before using a ballpoint pen? Or does it mean people wait until the ballpoint pen runs out of ink before they use it? No, it means that people lose ballpoint pens or stash them in a junk drawer: people rarely use up all the ink in a ballpoint pen.

## AVOID FANCY WORDS

If you don't have a thesaurus, do not buy one. If you have one, throw it away. Fancy words in the thesaurus can be tempting, but strange errors appear in proposals when writers, thinking they have overused a certain word, look for its synonym in the thesaurus. For example:

This summary pulls together the salient points of this proposal to help the busy reader.

*Salient* is derived from a verb that means to "jut out." Therefore, *salient* doesn't mean the important points, it means those that leap out at you. If they leaped out at you, you wouldn't need them pulled together in a summary.

*Viable* means living or capable of sustaining life. *Viable cells* is okay, but what is a viable corporation? And what in the world is a viable kill mechanism?

*Comprise* means to embrace or include. Thus the book comprises four volumes. The zoo comprises the animals. Our Statement of Work comprises four tasks (please, not *is comprised of*).

> Use familiar words—words that your readers will understand, and not words they will have to look up. No advice is more elementary, and no advice is more difficult to accept. When we feel an impulse to use a marvelously exotic word, let us lie down until the impulse goes away.
>
> —JAMES K. KILPATRICK, in *The Writer's Art*

> The difference between the right word and the almost right word is the difference between lightning and the lightning bug.
>
> —MARK TWAIN

Your objective is not to impress the proposal reviewer with big words, but to convey your meaning clearly. Remember, the reviewer is tired, distracted, and in a hurry to get your proposal off his or her desk. You can certainly play with big, wonderful words. Use them to win Scrabble games or to complete crossword puzzles. Don't use them in your proposal unless you want to puzzle your reader.

## RESIST USING TECHNICAL WORDS FROM ANOTHER FIELD

We're not talking about avoiding big technical words inherent in your field. If you are a chemist writing a proposal to the chemistry section of the National Science Foundation, the reviewers are not going to be stumped by words like ethylenediaminetetraacetic acid. They will probably even catch little jokes or puns on these words. I've heard chemists giggle about the poor fellow who fell in the esterification kettle and was horribly butylated. They guffaw over the bumper sticker "Old chemists never die; they just oxidize." Molecular physicists snicker when they read about metastable daughter ions clustered around their naked parents.

However, you need to be wary of words that have slid from one field to another and lost their meaning. For example:

- Mathematicians use *parameter* and *factor* to refer to special concepts.
- Scientists use *spectrum* and *mutate* for specific meanings.
- Computer specialists use *input* and *interface* correctly.
- Grammarians need *gender* and *nominal.*

A booklet distributed by the Environmental Protection Agency for its writers says:

When people use their own technical words correctly and in the proper context, those words are not offensive. They are necessary to communicate accurately. What happens, though, is that the sublanguages crossbreed, and the resulting hybrid becomes unintelligible to many readers.

When people borrow these hybrid words, they use *parameter* when they really mean *boundary* or *condition*. They write that they have *covered the whole spectrum of possibilities* when they really just mean *range*. They use *interface* as a verb. They write the *male gender* when they really mean the *male sex*.

Proposal reviewers will accept even complex technical words that are naturally used in the subject of the proposal. What will drive them up the wall is use of words that are unclear for the subject you are discussing or fancy for no good reason, except to show off.

## QUIT TRYING TO IMPRESS YOUR READER

Trying to impress your reader with your writing style is like trying to be funny. The harder you try, the less you'll succeed. Here's what happened to one writer when he focused on style rather than content:

> Of concern here is the extent to which the need (legal) for scientifically derived evidence and the ability of criminalists to provide this evidence has resulted generally in the fact that a particular crime category is viewed as significant to the extent that (a) there are legal requirements for the presentation of scientifically derived physical evidence and (b) there exists the capability for accurately and efficiently developing analyses of physical evidence.
>
> Perhaps a specific example will clarify the nature of our concern. . . .

Perhaps not.

Here's another that sounds like a civil servant at work:

> Final inspection of the product encompasses the accumulation of many variables up to the time an item is presented for final inspection prior to packaging and return to the preparation room or forwarding to its next designation. It is at this point that the completed documentation package is reviewed, verified for completeness and traceability accuracy and recompiled as required before physical packaging or protective wrapping. Visual and measured inspection of the item is checked to assure compliance.

What is it that's wrong with this style of writing? Why is it so hard to understand? Chuck Scarlet, a technical editor in Silicon Valley in the early sixties, described the difference between "hard" and "easy" writing:

> "Hard" writing is generally removed from the way we naturally talk. It's elaborate, Latinized, dandified, and complex. "Easy" writing is not necessarily the same as good writing. However, "easy" writing usually does a better job of conveying meaning than its more complicated counterpart. The idea that "hard" writing is more exact, more precise, more compact, is widely held—but manifestly incorrect.

Scarlet gave this example, posted in many business offices in New York City during the enforced blackouts of World War II:

> Illumination is required to be extinguished before these premises are closed to business.

Everyone would understand it better as, "Last one out, turn out the lights."

But my proposal is highly technical, you say. Shouldn't it sound like the journals in my field? No. Your journal articles can sound as stuffy as they please, but a proposal needs to be simply presented. It *can* be done, even with highly technical subjects.

For example, the subject of the earth's ozone problems can be discussed in intricate scientific detail. Even in news articles, I never understood why one article would say that scientists are worried about a hole in the ozone layer and another would say they're worried about too much ozone. Here's the complex subject of ozone described very simply by Dave Crosley, director of a group that does research on lasers and sensors, to clarify the distribution of ozone to the European Parliament:

> Ozone is a special, chemically active form of oxygen containing three oxygen atoms and has the chemical formula $O_3$. Most of it lies in the ozone layer, a region of enhanced concentration lying at altitudes between 10 and 40 km in the stratosphere, and it plays crucial roles in the Earth's environment. Most important is its beneficial absorption of much solar ultraviolet radiation.

Ozone is also present in the troposphere, below 10 km altitude, where it has very different environmental characteristics. Here it is found at far lower concentrations than in the stratosphere, and it exhibits harmful qualities. Tropospheric ozone can damage materials and living tissue and is a component of urban smog.

It is stratospheric ozone, the topic of this proposal, that is beneficial to the earth's environment and that is endangered by human activities.

Look at how these short, direct sentences present this complex subject in easy stages. Look at the way the technical terms are always clarified by simpler terms. The only stumbling block for the American reader might be the use of kilometers, but kilometers were certainly appropriate for Crosley's European audience. If we convert kilometers to miles, we can see that the ozone high above the earth (from about six to twenty-five miles) protects us from too much ultraviolet radiation, so we want to keep it. The ozone near the earth (below six miles) damages life and causes smog, so we want less of it. Now, I've certainly oversimplified a complex subject, but Crosley's simple, direct writing finally helped me understand the issue.

Dick Meyers, manager of a publications group, talked about the objective of technical writing:

We should seek clarity and precision above all. We should also try, of course, to be as readable as possible and as graceful as possible; however, we will be doing excellently if we can simply be clear and precise.

Think about how you feel when you are reading for information and what you need to know is written in a lofty, sonorous style. Does it make you admire the writer or does it make you feel stupid? Doesn't it make you want to tell the writer to just come off it and explain it simply?

Iouri Balachov, a scientist from Russia, said it very well:

My son was writing the essay to go with his application to college. He was trying to impress the acceptance committee, but I told him not to try to impress them with big words. I said, just tell them honestly how you feel about attending their school. Say it as simply and clearly as you can.

His son was accepted.

Impress your audience with the innovation of your approach, with the clarity of your logic, yes. But don't try to impress them with your big vocabulary. It will backfire. At best, they will misunderstand you. At worst, they will stop reading.

> Have something to say and say it as clearly as you can. That is the only secret of style.
> —MATTHEW ARNOLD

## TIPS FOR SIMPLIFYING YOUR WRITING

You can simplify your writing by omitting needless words, avoiding fad redundancies, and avoiding fancy words, especially technical words from another field. Don't try to impress your audience, just try to be simple and clear. Here are some ways you can change your writing from complex to simple.

Replace wordy phrases with simple words:

| INSTEAD OF | USE |
| --- | --- |
| a number of | several |
| a substantial amount | many, much |
| on the order of | about |
| in order to | to |
| due to the fact that | because |
| in spite of the fact that | even though |
| during the course of | during |
| sufficiently fast | fast enough |
| in figure 1 is shown | figure 1 shows |
| it is my intention | I intend |
| used for fuel purposes | used for fuel |
| this is a subject that | This subject |
| the reason why is that | Because |

Delete or revise unnecessary opening phrases:

| CHANGE THIS | TO READ |
|---|---|
| It is to be noted that | Note that (or delete) |
| It may be seen that | (delete) |
| It is our understanding that | We understand that |
| It is thus evident that | Evidently (or delete) |
| It is not inconceivable that | (delete) |
| (e.g., It is not inconceivable that the door is blue.) | (The door may be blue.) |
| It is very likely that (the door is blue) | (delete) (The door is probably blue.) |
| One cannot exclude the possibility that . . . | (delete) (The door might be blue.) |
| It is apparent that | Apparently |
| One can see that | (delete) |
| There was no cognizance of the fact that | We (they) did not know (realize) |
| There has been an appreciation of the fact that | We (now) appreciate |
| One could have stated almost with certainty that | We thought/We predicted |
| One final point concerns the fact that | Finally |
| The reader is referred to | Please see |

Change redundant phrases to simple words:

| CHANGE THIS REDUNDANT PHRASE | TO READ |
|---|---|
| current status | status |
| potential candidate | candidate |
| in close proximity to | in proximity to [or] near |
| at the present time | at present [or] now |
| three different methods | three methods |
| free gift | gift |
| personal friend | friend |
| my personal opinion | my opinion |

| CHANGE THIS REDUNDANT PHRASE | TO READ |
|---|---|
| future plans | plans, future work |
| method of approach | approach |
| very unique | unique |

Replace fancy words or stuffy words with simple words:

| REPLACE THIS | WITH THIS |
|---|---|
| plethora | abundance |
| dearth | scarcity |
| commence, initiate | begin |
| prior to | before |
| subsequent to | after |
| subsequently | later [or] next |
| necessitate | require, need |
| employ | use |
| utilize | use |
| prioritize | set priorities, rank |
| hereinafter | later/from here on |
| implement | do |
| presently | soon |

# The Simplicity of a Zen Garden

## HOW TO RESCUE DOOMED SENTENCES, GROW STRONG VERBS, AND CLEAN UP AFTER YOURSELF

●

*That's not writing, that's typing.*

—TRUMAN CAPOTE, when Jack Kerouac boasted that he never changed a line

●

Here's a scene in a garden:

Harry suddenly sat bolt upright on the garden bench. He had been staring absent-mindedly into the hedge—*and the hedge was staring back.* Two enormous green eyes had appeared among the leaves.

That paragraph, from J. K. Rowling's *Harry Potter and the Chamber of Secrets,* is as clean and tidy as a paragraph can be. Nothing could be removed, and nothing needs to be added. It appears simple, but such a lot happens in a small space.

A Zen garden is also spare and appears simple. One tree, raked sand, a few large stones carefully set off from one another. Each item can be viewed separately. It is clean. No profusion of colors and shapes, no confusion. And it takes a lot of work to make it that simple.

Although a Zen garden is simple, it's not boring. Imagine a Zen garden in the rain. The raindrops plopping into the raked sand sound different from the rain dripping through the branches of the one small pine tree. And different again from the raindrops splattering on the

Revising is part of writing. Few writers are so expert that they can produce what they are after on the first try. . . . Do not be afraid to seize what you have written and cut it to ribbons; it can always be restored to its original condition in the morning.

—E. B. WHITE
in *The Elements of Style*

three boulders in one corner of the garden or rattling the small pebbles lining the path made of roughly square flat stones.

With a lot of work, your writing can be clean and spare yet interesting. This chapter covers three ways to refine your writing:

- How to rescue the sentence that was doomed from the beginning.
- How to grow strong sentences.
- How to clean up your writing as a courtesy to the readers.

## THE SENTENCE THAT WAS DOOMED FROM THE BEGINNING

James Thurber, in *The Ladies and Gentlemen's Guide to Modern English Usage*, describes a man who got himself into a sentence and never got out. It started innocently when the man and his wife went to call on another couple, but their friends were not at home. Planning to leave them a note of regret, the man writes:

"We would have liked to have found you in." Reading it over, the gentleman is assailed by the suspicion that he has too many "haves," and that the whole business has somehow been put too far into the past. His first reaction is to remedy this by dating the note: "9 p.m., Wednesday, Jan. 21, 1931." This at once seems too formal, and with a sigh he starts in again on the sentence itself. That is where he makes a fatal mistake. The simplest way out, as always, is to seek some other method of expressing the thought.

The man keeps struggling with the sentence, taking an envelope out of his pocket and grimly making a list of all the possible combinations.

At length he has the bright inspiration of going into the hope clauses and turns out: "We had hoped to have been able to have found." If he has married the right kind of woman, she will hastily scratch a brief word on a calling card, shove it under the door, and drag her husband away.

A bad sentence is like quicksand. If you find yourself trapped in one, thrashing about will only make it worse. Give up and start over.

"Write with nouns and verbs," says Strunk in *The Elements of Style*. "The adjective hasn't been invented that can pull a weak or inaccurate noun out of a tight place." That's one solution—take out the adjectives—but taking out adjectives won't solve the problem of this sentence:

In figure 3 are shown comparisons between our data and that of Jones, demonstrating that there is general experimental agreement, and that the sophistication of the theory appears to be at a level that one should be able to use calculated values for pressures that are experimentally unattainable.

The adjectives *our, general, experimental,* and *calculated* do useful work here and taking them out won't make the sentence clear.

Some sentences are just doomed from the beginning. You can recognize doomed sentences easily in other people's writing. They sound like this:

1. Accomplishment of the measurements is to be achieved by sequencing the metric system sequentially.
2. The manner of categorization will depend on the nature and volume of the data that are available.
3. It is to be expected that the forces needed to accomplish this mission will be forthcoming.
4. There is the possibility that achievement of the commercialization will be accomplished.
5. This is also an important factor which affects the choice of specimen size and geometry.

When you combine sentences of this type into a paragraph, you get government writing. Tell me what this paragraph means:

Cost and pricing data are not required in response to this solicitation because it is anticipated that the resultant contract award is at or below the cost or pricing data threshold (currently $500,000). A price analysis will be made by the Government to determine the reasonableness of the price and any need for further negotiation. Offerors are asked to submit information other than cost or pricing data in the Budget Summary format provided in Section J, attachment 3b, DOT for 4220.44. This is necessary in order to help establish price reasonableness or price realism.

Why is this paragraph so hard to understand? The words are not unusual. The sentences are not overly long or convoluted. But the meaning must be pried out like an oyster from its shell. Why?

## WHAT DOOMED SENTENCES HAVE IN COMMON

What do all these example sentences have in common? We shall see here just where the writers went wrong and how to switch onto a clearer path immediately.

First, look at the sentences numbered 1 through 5. What are the verbs in these sentences? *Is, will depend, is, is, is.* In the government paragraph, the verbs are *are required, will be made, are asked,* and *is.* So it seems to be a problem with verbs, and I know you've been told before to use strong verbs. In these doomed sentences, the writers have turned good verbs into nouns. I often see sentences that start out:

Measurement of the temperature has been accomplished by . . .
Adjustment of the openings enabled us to . . .
Identification of the key will allow . . .

Strong verbs like *measure, adjust,* and *identify* have been turned into vague nouns that function as the subjects of indirect and wordy sentences. These sentences make the reader work harder to understand what you mean.

On second look, verbs aren't really the root of the problem. The writers of sentences numbered 1 through 5 first went wrong by choosing weak subjects: *accomplishment, manner, it, there,* and *this.* Yes, those *are* the grammatical subjects of those sentences. Because those subjects are so vague, the verbs can't hold them up, and the whole sentence starts to sink.

If you start with strong, tangible words as subjects, your sentences will lift up their heads and sing. Again, let's hear from *Harry Potter:*

The teapot went berserk and squirted boiling tea all over the place and one man ended up in the hospital with the sugar tongs clamped to his nose.

Or, even better:

A glass case nearby held a withered hand on a cushion, a blood-stained pack of cards, and a staring glass eye. Evil-looking masks stared down from the walls, an assortment of human bones lay upon the counter, and rusty, spiked instruments hung from the ceiling. Even worse, the dark, narrow street Harry could see through the dusty shop window was definitely not Diagon Alley.

Hoo boy, these are strong subjects! (My entire family—kids and grown-ups—have become enthralled with Harry Potter books, reading parts out loud to each other, nagging each other to hurry up and finish the next volume.)

## OVERCOMING THE FEAR OF ACTIVE VERBS

Some writers seem to fear active verbs and verb forms. Instead of writing,

Just as the sun set over the ocean, the pirates returned to the ship carrying casks of gold.

the verb-fearing writer writes:

The setting of the sun over the ocean was seen to occur in coincidence with the return of the pirates to the ship, their arms in support of casks of gold.

Well, why not? The meaning is the same, isn't it? Yes, but it's much harder to grasp quickly, and everything is indirect instead of direct. When people read for information—as opposed to reading to be mystified or moved to tears or sexually excited—they want the sentence to be in a form that is most easily decoded. That form is subject, verb, object:

The batter hit the ball.
The frog jumped into the pond.

Your readers can still translate what you mean if you present this information in passive form:

> Hitting of the ball was achieved by the batter.
> Jumping into the pond was accomplished by the frog.

But it's more work, and they won't thank you for it. Here, instead of active verbs (*hit* and *jumped*), we have passive verbs (*was achieved* and *was accomplished*). The subjects of the sentence no longer *do* anything; they have things done to them. The passive construction has blunted all the action of the sentences and blurred the easily decoded form of subject, verb, object.

What I see in a lot of scientific writing makes the reader do even more decoding:

> Achievement of ball hitting was effected by the batter.
> Levitation into the lentic water body was accomplished by the *Diplasiocoela.*

These sentences are two steps removed from "The batter hit the ball" or "The frog jumped into the pond." They are not just passive, they've surrendered.

You may well believe that the grammar checker on your computer will take care of this problem. Hah! Here's how my grammar checker suggested fixing the two sentences above:

> The batter effected achievement of ball hitting.
> The *Diplasiocoela* accomplished levitation into the lentic water body.

The grammar checker, bless its little heart, was doing its best by changing the sentence from passive voice to active voice, but that just wasn't enough to save it from doom.

## HOW TO GROW STRONG SENTENCES

Where do you start to strengthen your own weak sentences? With the grammatical subject. The grammatical subject of the sentence below is *dissolution* and the verb is *was achieved:*

> Dissolution of the tablet was achieved in water.

Find a real, tangible object in this sentence to use as the grammatical subject, and you have:

The tablet dissolved in water.

Now, the sentence is easily decoded. The subject is tangible, and the verb is active. To be really daring in today's business and scientific writing, try taking it one step further:

We dissolved the tablet in water.

A change like this may not seem earthshaking for this single sentence, but making this kind of change throughout your proposal will sharpen and tighten it, keeping bored, tired reviewers absorbing your information easily.

Try rewriting this doozy by finding a tangible word to replace the vague subject *it:*

It is our opinion that, because labeling of compounds has already been accomplished, further effort is unnecessary.

You may start by eliminating needless words to change "It is our opinion that" to "Our opinion is that." That's a good beginning, but it's not enough because we still have an intangible subject *our opinion* and that boring verb *is.* As usual with passive sentences, the people who hold the opinion are absent, so you need to create them. Start out bravely with *we:*

We believe further work is unnecessary because the compounds have already been labeled.

The sentence is now easily translated, and you saved four words.

Nine years before Niels Bohr won the Nobel Prize in physics, he wrote to his brother Harald, "It could be that I've perhaps found out a little bit about the structure of atoms." What a weak, hesitant sentence that is, we are thinking. But read on to the last sentence of his letter: "You can imagine how anxious I am to finish quickly." Now we can see his first sentence as barely concealed exhilaration, excitement tempered by humility.

When we first have a great idea, we are reluctant to say it boldly, so we write sentences that begin, "It is likely that . . ." or, "It may be possible that . . ." or, "There exists the likelihood that . . ." Wimp city. Rewrite them.

## TIME TO CLEAN UP YOUR WRITING

You've written the first draft of your proposal. It may be magnificent or it may be dreadful, but before you show it to your first reader, you need to clean it up. Even if your first reader is your best friend, it's courteous and workmanlike to clear away the debris.

When I was trying to sell our first house—a fifty-year-old gracious lady in need of a face lift—I made the beds, swept the floor, and made the house as clean and shining as possible. The rug in the living room had a big grape juice stain, so before each prospective buyer arrived, I laid out the Sunday funnies on the floor, making it appear a child had just been shooed away from reading there.

Putting the funnies on the floor didn't fix the stained rug and sweeping the house didn't replace the old plumbing, but the house was presented in its best light. That's what we're going to do for your proposal here. Make it clean and tidy for the first readers. Give them a clean path for finding your glaring errors, faults of logic, and passages no one can understand.

Cleaning up your writing should include at least these four steps:

- Checking its appearance on the page.
- Checking spelling and word usage.
- Checking for subject and verb agreement.
- Changing passive sentences to active voice.

When I was first an editor, I couldn't keep all these checkpoints in my mind at one time, so I went through each proposal a separate time for each item. Once for spelling, then for subject/verb agreement, and so on. Do it that way this first time.

## Checking Your Proposal's Appearance

To see problems you never saw on the computer screen, print the proposal and turn the pages slowly.

- Are the margins wide enough?
- Are the headings consistent? Do they show the true hierarchy of your proposal's organization?

- Does the page appear as a big block of text, or are there paragraph breaks at least every ten or twelve lines?
- Could you break up certain large blocks of text with bulleted lists?
- Do the headings and paragraph breaks (topic sentences) lead the reader to know what will come next?

Many writers let the reader know what's coming next by including road maps:

This section of the proposal describes four new ideas we will examine.

A road map is not a bad idea, but it can be overdone, especially if every section starts out, "This section describes . . ." You end up writing a proposal about the proposal instead of about your proposed work. One proposal actually said:

This section gives a road map of the four new ideas in our proposal.

A more graceful version of that sentence might be the following:

The proposed work will test four new ideas: (1) [and so on]

Watch out for road maps given at the *end* of a section announcing the next section. The writer is thinking of what's coming next, but the reader may not read straight through the proposal and will miss that transition unless it's at the *beginning* of the new section. Remember, most reviewers don't read straight through. They may read the first section of four proposals at a time, then the second sections, and so on.

## Checking Spelling and Word Use

You would think we no longer have any excuse for typos or misspelled words, now that computers all have spell checking programs. But the problem still lies with the computer user. Don't okay that word too fast. If the computer can't suggest a correct spelling, you'll have to do it the old-fashioned way: look it up.

As you've certainly noticed, spelling checkers can also approve words that are wrong. I've been curious why my spelling checker would pass right over the misspelling of *posses* for *possess*. Aha, it thinks *posses* is the plural of *posse*, as in "Let's go git 'em, cowboys."

One thing spelling checkers cannot tell you is whether it's the right word for that sentence. Careful manual proofreading will catch from/form, if/it, its/it's, there/their errors. One way to find these errors is to read your proposal over backward.

To avoid distracting your reader, you need to catch other kinds of words regularly misused. The most common errors I see are confusing *effect* with *affect;* misusing *ensure, insure,* and *assure;* and confusing *principle* with *principal:*

- *Effect* is a noun, *affect* is a verb: One effect of a drought is a forest fire, which affects small animals.
- *Assure* means to convey comfort (assurance), *insure* is to provide financial coverage, and *ensure* means to guarantee: My agent assured me that my house is insured for enough to ensure financial recovery of its cost.
- *Principal* is the main one; *principle* is a guiding idea or theory: The principal investigator will examine the principle of cold fusion.

A good source for learning about word usage is Theodore Bernstein's *The Careful Writer.* Words often misused are listed in alphabetical order. A shorter version that will also help you get over the things you thought your schoolteacher taught you is Bernstein's *Miss Thistlebottom's Hobgoblins*—all the rules you can now break without feeling guilty.

## Checking for Subject/Verb Agreement

Well, this seems too obvious to worry about, doesn't it? But when the subject and verb are far apart, many a writer slips up, as in this sentence:

The problem of determining the sequence of decisions that do *not* lead to complete failure of businesses are distinct from, and much more difficult than, the problem of determining the decisions that lead to success.

If you can find your way back to the subject, *problem,* you will find you need to change the verb from *are* to *is.*

In sentences doomed from the outset, the verb arrives so late and so far from the subject, with so much hogwash intervening, that by the time the writer reaches the verb, he has long ago forgotten not only what the subject was, but what the sentence is trying to say. As in the sentence you just read and in the sentence below (I've put the subject and the verb in italics):

A preliminary analysis *procedure* for assessing potential environmental damage to aquatic biota, which incorporates the most appropriate methodologies used to determine chronic and acute toxicity of aquatic organisms and the frequency-duration probability prediction procedures developed in the early phase of the proposed study, *were developed*.

Here, the writer must abandon the sentence and start over: "We developed a preliminary analysis procedure . . ."

Some words like *media, criteria,* and *data* sound singular but are really plural. Remember, it's

one medium, two media
one criterion, two criteria
one datum, two data

Words like *headquarters* sound plural but are singular. Your company has only one headquarters.

## Changing Passive to Active

If you've used the grammar checker on your computer, you know how often it snidely asks you: "Did you mean to use passive voice here?" But how does it know?

You can spot passive constructions in your sentences by looking for verb forms like *was done* and *was made*. Look for nouns having things done to them, as in, "The streetlight was smashed into by the car." Watch for verbs ending in "-ed," as in, "The bill was approved by Congress." or "The buffet was devoured by the partygoers." (My editor reminded me that doing a search for the word *by* is also a good flag for passive constructions.)

For good examples of *active* verbs, consider sports writing:

Rogers sidestepped Williams to slide into home plate in the last inning. The Bulls triumphed over the Bears by 7 points.

In passive voice, it would read:

> Williams was sidestepped by Rogers and home plate was slid into in the last inning. The Bears were triumphed over by the Bulls by 7 points.

Passive voice often hides the person or thing that performed the action. For example:

> Williams was sidestepped and home plate was slid into in the last inning. The Bears were triumphed over by 7 points.

Yes, but who won the game?

Passive voice dilutes your writing and makes it wordy, but it's not forbidden. Here are two *good* uses for passive voice:

1. When you need to be tactful or discreet. After a dreadful Forty Niner game in the seventies, in which Jerry Rice dropped three clean passes from Joe Montana, Coach Walsh said on the television news: "Mistakes were made in the game today." Walsh is a nice guy.
2. When you are describing an experiment or a process. The American Institute of Physics encourages active writing (even saying "we" and "I") but approves of a sentence like "Air was admitted to the chamber." As they say, "Who cares who turned the valve?"

## AN EXERCISE FOR MAKING YOUR WRITING STRONGER

Go through your proposal and circle every sentence that has *it* or *this* or *there* as the grammatical subject. Now circle each sentence that uses a fuzzy, intangible noun as the subject. Rewrite each sentence by finding the true, solid subject and a strong verb to go with it. For example:

| CHANGE THIS | TO THIS |
| --- | --- |
| It is possible that the lottery may be won by me. | I may win the lottery |
| There were snakes writhing in the grass. | Snakes writhed in the grass. |
| This is exceedingly important in becoming king. | To become king, you need to . . . |
| Utilization of care is needed when lighting a bonfire. | Be careful when lighting a bonfire. |
| It is necessary that we pay taxes. | We must pay taxes. |
| One aspect of his face was an enormous nose. | His nose was enormous. |

Post these reminders on your computer or on the bulletin board over your desk:

- Sentences with tangible subjects and active verbs are easier to understand.
- Using strong subjects leads to stronger verbs.
- Strong subjects and verbs lead to shorter, clearer sentences.

# Haiku Are All Nuance

**14**

## WHY YOU NEED AN ANAL-RETENTIVE EDITOR

●

*No one spoke*
*The host, the guest,*
*The white chrysanthemums.*

—RYOTA, as translated by Kenneth Rexroth

●

We recognize haiku whether we find them in books of Japanese poetry or as computer error messages in haiku form posted on the Internet:

Rather than a beep
Or a rude error message,
These words: "File not found."

With searching comes loss
And the presence of absence:
"My Novel" not found.

First snow,
Then silence
This thousand-dollar screen dies

Yesterday it worked
Today it is not working
Windows is like that.

In the traditional Japanese haiku, all is nuance and allusion, as in this ancient haiku by Basho:

An old pond—
The sound
Of a diving frog.

Haiku are meant to give the reader a Zen-like flash of an image that is beyond the words on the page. In Jack Kerouac's *The Dharma Bums*, the character Japhy Ryder says:

A real haiku's gotta be as simple as porridge and yet make you see the real thing, like the greatest haiku of them all probably is the one that goes "The sparrow hops along the veranda, with wet feet." By Shiki. You see the wet footprints like a vision in your mind and yet in those few words you also see all the rain that's been falling that day and almost smell the wet pine needles.

## POETRY AND NUANCE WON'T SELL YOUR IDEAS

If you can make your proposal "as simple as porridge," you will be doing very well. But you cannot assume that the reader will unravel the subtle nuances of your proposal or see the same vision you intended unless the proposal actually states your ideas explicitly. The problem is that what seems absolutely clear to you as the writer may be as inexplicable as a haiku to your reader. And once the proposal leaves your hands, you cannot be there with your reader to correct any misinterpretation.

Here's a passage that appears as simple as porridge:

Experimental work has been limited by the lack of explosives and the existence of a test site. Both of these problems are now corrected.

Do you get the meaning the writer intended, or do you envision an exploding test site?

The writer of a book proposal on treatment of drug addiction would be surprised at his reader's reaction to this passage:

Ideally, methadone is mixed with fruit juice (to make injection difficult if the drug is stolen) and administered under the eyes of doctors or nurses.

Ouch!

Why couldn't the writers see the problems in these passages? Because they were too close to the writing. By the time you have written and revised and corrected your proposal, you could probably recite it in your sleep. At this stage, no matter how many times you go over the proposal, your eye will gloss over that terse allusion to your theory to read what you expect to see. You will see the vision of what you believe you have written, not necessarily what is actually on the page. Now you need a fresh eye. You need someone to look at the proposal who does not love it or hate it. Someone who can find the soft spots that you thought were so solid.

## THE EDITOR'S EYE

What you need now is an anal-retentive editor. Technical editors and copy editors would be among the first to say that the phrase *anal-retentive editor* is redundant. All good editors take professional pride in being anal, although they prefer to consider themselves *careful* rather than *picky*.

A good editor is constantly catching errors everywhere, not just in your proposal. An editor heard the following statement in a newscast about a power slowdown in Britain:

> Hospital authorities have announced that, if the power is not turned back on, an operating table victim will die.

She shouted back to the television, "What do you *mean,* 'an operating table victim'? Is that someone who was hit by a gurney?" In proposals, editors ask: "What do you *mean,* 'the five-inch gun crew'? Is that a gun operated by very short people?"

Most editors are physically uncomfortable until they can get up and correct the spelling of a word on a flip-chart at the front of the room. They check restaurant menus for errors before they decide what to order. Technical editors have to shift gears when they read a novel to stop checking for agreement of subject and verb. They catch typos even in sexy passages.

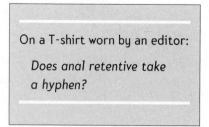

On a T-shirt worn by an editor:

*Does anal retentive take a hyphen?*

Good editors are narrow and focused. If you want to tease an editor, call one up and say, "I have a question we need resolved here. Is it 'nine plus one *is* eleven' or 'nine plus one *are* eleven'?" Like me, most editors will fall for it and go blathering on about whether you mean the *sum* of nine and one (which *is* eleven) or the *accumulation* of nine items and one item (which *are* equal to eleven). You *will* need to interrupt to remind her that nine plus one is *ten*.

Editors know a lot of good stuff that no one else cares to know. They know how to spell *meniscus* and *desiccate*. (I will *never* forget how to spell meniscus because I once let it slip by misspelled in six monthly reports before deciding to look it up.) They know tricks for remembering how to spell *pusillanimous* and *pharaoh* and *Philippines*. Editors know that *van der Waals* doesn't take an apostrophe and that *Dr Pepper* doesn't need a period.

Editors know that singular words that end in "s" still need an apostrophe when they're possessive: Charles's tonsils, Joan Rivers's humor. Editors know the difference between being eager and being anxious. Editors know that Rollerblade is a brand name: they won't let you write that you went *Rollerblading*, but they will let you go *in-line skating*.

Editors will be frustrated by the instructions on the package for Kellogg's Frosted Pop-Tarts with Real Blueberry Filling. (See the sidebar.)

To make all the instructions grammatically parallel, they will change instruction number 4 to read "Be careful when removing hot pastries from the toaster." And for heaven's sake, change "Supervise heating by children" to "Supervise children when they are heating pastries."

Editors have collections of sentences that make them laugh out loud. Here's what an editor would consider an amazingly understated warning about the hazards of noise:

> Some people damage their ears still further by pursuing loud hobbies. Every time a gun goes off in a hunter's ear, for example, it takes a few hearing cells with it.

Here are some peculiarly limited fires noted by editors:

> He taught an introductory course in combustion phenomena with major emphasis on unwanted fires at the University of Minnesota from 1965 through 1968.

## Toasting Instructions

1. Set toaster at low or light heat—drop pastry in vertically.
2. Attend toaster while heating.
3. Supervise heating by children.
4. Care should be used when removing hot pastries from the toaster.

The marshall keeps records of all fires started by pyromaniacs in his desk drawer.

Here's a passage that seems to show the hazards of being a broker:

Valuable punched cards listing shareholders and their holdings were the prizes sought by ambitious brokers combing streets in the Los Angeles financial district after being thrown out windows during the New Year's celebration.

Editors treasure unintended images like this one in a proposal to develop a new fiber for disposable diapers:

Product development for adult incontinence is still in its infancy, but many industry experts believe that, as baby boomers become senior citizens, we will enter the golden age of incontinence.

## SCIENCE AS A SECOND LANGUAGE: WHAT TECHNICAL EDITORS LOOK FOR

Harold Ross, the first managing editor of *The New Yorker*, admonished his editors to "try to preserve an author's style if he is an author and has a style." An editor will first turn through the pages of your proposal to get a feel for its structure and organization. Does it seem logical and sensible? If the proposal responds to a Request for Proposal, does it meet all the requirements of the RFP? Does it respond to all the evaluation criteria? Is it organized the way the reviewers will expect to find it? Does it meet the page limits?

An editor will check the proportions of the proposal. If sections two, three, and four are about 10 pages each and section five is 120 pages, maybe something is wrong. Perhaps section five should be broken up into several sections, or perhaps most of it should really be an appendix.

Dick Meyers, manager of the publications group where I started editing, gave editors this advice:

> Editors are best when writers barely
> know they exist,
> Not so good when writers always
> obey and acclaim them,
> Worst when writers despise them.
> With good editors, when their work
> is done and their aims fulfilled,
> The writer will say, "I did this myself."
> —Paraphrase of Lao-tsu
> in *The Body Language and Emotion
> of Cats* by M. M. Milani

If everything seems to be satisfactory (superficially), start detailed textual editing; if something seems seriously awry (even if you can't precisely pinpoint it), talk to the author about your questions and misgivings. He may very well tell you that you're technically unqualified to have an opinion, but he may also say something like "I knew something was wrong, but I didn't know what." One of the greatest contributions an editor can make is to point out the "soft spots" in a manuscript—and major flaws in structure and organization are very soft spots indeed.

A good editor will also look for the smaller soft spots such as the wrong word, the jargon, the awkward sentence, the muddy paragraph, the lack of proper transition, the illogical development of a section, redundancy and windiness, and the lack of sufficient information. While doing all this, the editor will be checking spelling, fixing dangling constructions, making sure all abbreviations are defined, making sure the headings are consistent with the structure of the proposal, and making sure all tables and figures and references are numbered correctly.

Meyers advised editors to make these changes gracefully:

> As a matter of tactics, it's a good idea to make changes provisionally. We are not grading papers, after all, and we are not trying to show the author how stupid he is; we are trying—with the author and his supervisors—to produce the best possible proposal we can. On a noncritical point, I would tend to yield to the author; on something that is clearly wrong, though, I would stand fast.

## THE MYSTERY OF *WHICH* AND *THAT*

Editors not only know the difference between *which* and *that*, they also know a secret way to deal with them. First, the difference. The style manual for the Council of Biology Editors states:

Precise usage favors *that* to introduce a restrictive (defining, limiting) clause and *which* to introduce a nonrestrictive (nondefining), descriptive clause. Maintaining the distinction between these relative pronouns contributes to clarity and ready understanding.

Big help, huh?

Here's another way to explain it: Use *that* if the sentence must include that clause (phrase) to make a full statement:

This is the house that Jack built last summer.

If you could put the clause (phrase) in parenthesis or take it out of the sentence without changing the overall meaning, use *which*.

This is Jack's red house, which he built last summer.

Here are some more examples, where the words are exactly the same but the meanings are different:

| | |
|---|---|
| The tests that failed are not included in this report. | The tests, which failed, are not included in this report. |
| The bottles that exploded were swept under the rug. | The bottles, which exploded, were swept under the rug. |

The sentences on the left mean that only some of the tests failed or only some of the bottles exploded. Those *that* failed or exploded were excluded or swept under the rug. The sentences on the right mean that all the tests failed and all the bottles exploded.

Why does it matter? Because it helps your reader understand. Try following either of these directions as if you would be sent to jail if you did it wrong:

Library books which are worn and tattered should be discarded.
Throw towels which are dirty into the tub.

Do you throw away all library books and throw all towels in the tub? No. Using *that* would make these sentences clear.

Library books that are worn and tattered should be discarded.
Throw towels that are dirty into the tub.

Now we get to the secret editors know about *which* and *that*. Most of the time, you can simply do away with *which* and *that* by rewriting the sentence:

Discard all worn and tattered library books.
Throw dirty towels in the tub.

Try your hand at eliminating *which* or *that* in these sentences:

We believe that we can build a better birdhouse.
The apparatus is composed of two chambers, which are designated A and B.
Table 1 lists the metals that were tested in this project.
A package that has been subjected to post office abuse will suffer damage.

The resulting sentences have not lost any of the original meaning:

We believe we can build a better birdhouse.
The apparatus is composed of two chambers, designated A and B.
Table 1 lists the metals tested in this project.
A package subjected to post office abuse will suffer damage.

Sometimes you need to recast the sentence to delete *that* or *which*, but the result is a tighter sentence. For example:

There are some transitions in the baseline of the mixture that will need to be examined later.

Here you need to fiddle with it a little to produce

Some transitions in the baseline of the mixture will need to be examined later.

See how rewriting to eliminate a *that* can tighten a sentence? Try revising the following sentences before you look at the answers on page 152.

These are the compounds that are likely to give the best monopropellant
formulations.

This is a field that is in its infancy.

This is the project that was overrun by $100,000.

## WHAT EDITORS IGNORE

Proposal writers often tell editors, "This proposal won't take you long. Most of
it has been already been edited." Editors always ignore this advice, and writers
never understand why. Proposal writers seem particularly curious why editors
insist on reediting "the boilerplate"—the standard parts of the proposal such as
qualification statements, lists of facilities and equipment, and the standard
description of the company. Proposal writers shake their heads and ponder:
"Why is it you can put the same boilerplate section through editing over and
over, and every time they will find more things to change?" Here's one attempt
to explain it.

### WHY EDITORS REEDIT THE BOILERPLATE

- Although the boilerplate has been edited many times before, the authors
  never insert the edited version in the new proposal, preferring to use their
  untouched, virgin version.
- Editors like to sit around telling war stories about the time they found the
  wrong client's name in the boilerplate.
- Editors, like nurses, are trained in triage: they focus their energies on the
  paragraphs that have some chance of actually conveying meaning.
- Like car mechanics and surgeons, editors tend to say, "While we were in
  there, we thought we might as well fix the . . ."
- Boilerplate, like other matter, is subject to entropy. If left unattended for
  more than seventy-two hours, it reverts to its original disordered state.

And now for the number one reason editors reedit the boilerplate:

- The last three times this boilerplate was edited, it was in a five-hundred-
  page proposal written by twelve authors, and it was given to the editor in

bits and pieces, sent in two hundred seventy separate files, of which the boilerplate reached the editor only thirty-two seconds before the proposal was due to FedEx.

●

## FROM HAIKU TO CLARITY

- In the hard work of writing and revising a proposal, your clear vision may get as cloudy as a haiku.
- Now it's time to let an editor look it over.
- The editor will read it cold, the way your ultimate reader will read it.
- If there's a chance for misunderstanding, a good editor will find it before the proposal goes out to your client.

## Answers

Possible ways of revising sentences to eliminate a *that*.

These compounds are likely to give the best monopropellant formulations.
This field is in its infancy.
This project was overrun by $100,000.

PART
FOUR

# SATORI

Presenting Your Ideas

in Person

# Lions and Tigers and Bears, Oh My!

## 15

## USING *WU WEI* TO DIFFUSE STAGE FRIGHT

There will come a time when you need to tell your story—present your idea in person. You could be meeting the top executive of your company to sell your cost-saving idea. You could be pitching your book idea to an agent or pitching for survival of your innovative technology to a venture capitalist.

Some people actually like giving presentations. "At least it's easier than writing," they tell me. But for many of us, giving a presentation goes something like this: Your heart is pounding. Your ice-cold hands are shaking. Your mouth is filled with cotton, and your stomach is in a hard knot. Are you over the Atlantic in an airplane that just dropped two thousand feet? Are you standing before a firing squad? No, you are the next person to stand up and speak before a group of fifteen business associates. Why such irrational fear?

Well, because it's irrational. The *Wu Wei* approach to diffusing this irrational fear is not to fight against it, but to neutralize the fear by yielding to it. In *The Tao of Pooh,* Benjamin Hoff describes the nonaction *Wu Wei* approach to conflict solving in the Taoist martial art tai chi chuan:

> The *Wu Wei* principle underlying *T'ai Chi Ch'üan* can be understood by striking at a piece of cork floating in water. The harder you hit it, the more it yields; the more it yields, the harder it bounces back. Without expending energy, the cork can easily wear you out. So, *Wu Wei* overcomes force by neutralizing its power, rather than by adding to the conflict.

# THE GROUP DYNAMICS OF STAGE FRIGHT

*The Book of Lists* gives the fourteen worst human fears, as reported by the *Sunday Times*, London (October 7, 1973). A team of market researchers asked three thousand people in the United States: "What are you the most afraid of?" Many named more than one, and 41 percent of them gave "speaking before a group" as number one. Way down in sixth place was death. Twice as many people were afraid of speaking in public as were afraid of dying. So, death is only remotely disturbing, but speaking in front of others scares the pants off us.

Why do so many people fear speaking before a group more than they fear death, war, prison, disease, Stephen King novels, or driving on the freeway? I think Woody Allen hit on something important:

> Death is one of the few things that can be done as easily lying down. The difference between sex and death is that, with death, you can do it alone and no one is going to make fun of you.

Let's look at it this way:

> From age thirteen to thirty, you worry about what other people will think about you. From thirty to fifty, you don't care what others think about you. After fifty, you realize nobody is thinking about you.
> —ANONYMOUS

Our worst fear is not really speaking in front of a group. It's the fear of being laughed at—of being ridiculed.

Over a lifetime, we invest intense energy to avoid looking like a silly fool in front of the whole village. Every morning, for example, we get up and put on clothes. Civilization has refined this fear to the point that people can now feel publicly humiliated simply because their clothes are made of a different type of cloth. Say, taffeta when everyone else is wearing denim. Or polyester, when the in-people are wearing natural fibers.

Even nudists, who would seem to be exceptionally brave, aren't really. They've simply learned the secret of getting everyone to do the same silly thing at the same time so nobody looks foolish. Think about people wearing bibs in a lobster restaurant. We don't seem to mind being foolish if the whole village is being foolish, but alone in front of the group? No way.

## A GRADUAL CURE

Psychologists are now successfully treating people who have irrational fears, such as fear of heights or fear of spiders, by a gradual approach. In a safe, controlled setting, the person is brought gently closer to experiencing the thing they fear. Are you afraid of spiders? *Yesssss!* Can you look at one in an enclosed box? *Nooooooo.* Can you look at a picture of a spider? No. Can you say the word *spider?* Maybe. Okay, we start there.

Fear of speaking in front of a group can be diffused in the same way. But, hey, if you're reading this while waiting in the green room to appear on the *Today* show, you'll just have to wing it. This diffusing needs to be done in slow stages.

And although this fear of speaking before others is top rated, many people have survived giving presentations. Some people even do it for a living. How? By accepting the fear. You can't force yourself to be calm, and you can't just ignore it, hoping it will go away.

What you *can* do is divert the force of the fear against the fear itself, as in the martial arts. Akido, for example, is based on the idea of using your attacker's energy rather than your own. Rather than push back against the force of your attackers, you divert their energy to send them flying over your head. Here are the first steps in diverting your fear of public speaking:

- Recognize the symptoms of speech terror.
- Observe them.
- Accept them.

Let's look at how it works and some techniques for making it happen.

## Recognizing the Symptoms of Speech Terror

The first time I had to speak in front of a large audience, I was the leader of a women's group at my company. We announced a meeting to explain the laws against discrimination in the workplace, and we encouraged men as well as women to attend. We expected a small turnout, but people were sitting in the aisles and standing in the doorways.

When someone gave me a handheld microphone, I had to put it down because my hand was shaking so hard that the microphone amplified my vibrations. So I stood behind the mike at the lectern, and because I am a very short person, no one could see much more than the top of my head. Being hidden by the lectern was just fine with me. My mouth went so dry, I had trouble moving my lips. Although there was a pitcher of water and a glass on the lectern, I didn't dare try to pour the water and lift the glass to my mouth.

What was happening to my body? You know about the adrenaline rush brought on by fear. In the days of early cave people, this body response could save lives. If you come out of your cave and find yourself face-to-face with a tiger, you need energy *now*. Your body charges itself up to give you all the energy and alertness you need to either kill that tiger or run like hell. Today, we seldom meet lions and tigers and bears head on, but when the brain sends out that message of fear, the rest of the body still kicks in with a full red alert.

Here's the thing:

Over millions of years, those humans who had good, strong red alert systems were the ones who survived long enough to be your ancestors.

You have to respect this system. Your body has been *programmed* to supercharge your whole central nervous system. You can't change it, so why not just learn to understand it?

## Observing Yourself in a State of Terror

Just observing these symptoms can help. When I was waiting to hear from my agent whether any publisher would bid on this book—and if they did, whether they would bid more than $2.98—I told my friend Fran I couldn't remember being so anxious since the last time I was waiting to find out if I was pregnant. Any of you remember that? You're not sure whether the news will be elating or dismaying, but you want to know *now*.

Fran, a courageous lady, told me, "Just observe yourself. Watch yourself being tense and anxious. Don't judge it, just observe it." Say, look at that, my hands are shaking. Say, listen to that heart of mine pounding away. Say, boy, am I feeling sick.

Observing these symptoms as a normal physiological response will not make them go away, but it will help you stay in the red alert stage and not accelerate to the full panic attack, which is really just being afraid of being afraid.

Being scared out of your wits is not so bad. You can still pretty much function. What does us in is becoming scared that people will *know* we're scared. But hear this and believe it: The audience won't notice nearly as much as you think. They may not even be able to tell you're scared witless. Mostly they'll be thankful *you're* up there instead of them.

Whatever you do as a speaker:

* Don't tell them you're scared.
* Don't ask them to forgive you in advance for being nervous.

I've seen speakers do both, and the audience resents it. Your fear is not their problem, and it's not their job to forgive you. Just go on speaking and soon you'll be okay.

## Accepting Your Terror

Professional speakers and actors who seem so at ease have simply become comfortable with their terror. Oh, they still have jumpy stomachs and the rush of fast heartbeats. They have them every time they appear in public. Every. Single. Time.

Vita, an actress, told me she has a recurring dream. "I am standing in the wings waiting to go on stage when I realize I don't know my lines. Now, that's nothing. It happens before every performance. But in the dream, I realize I don't even know what *play* we are performing!" Vita says that when she isn't at least

In his book *Peace Is Every Step*, Thich Nhat Hanh suggests an exercise: "Breathing in, I calm my body. Breathing out, I smile." He says we can recover ourselves completely after three breaths like this.

nervous before a performance, her performance isn't very good. She *uses* that adrenaline. She draws on that source of energy and harnesses it to make her performance sparkle.

## SOME TECHNIQUES FOR DIFFUSING YOUR RED ALERT SYSTEM

Without much effort, in a simple do-nothing *Wu Wei* mode, you can diffuse your red alert system by

- finding your center.
- visualizing your success.
- shortening the time you are scared.
- imagining it's over.

### Find Your Center

One of the techniques of achieving serenity in Eastern arts such as akido and tai chi is to find your center. Surprisingly, some Western sports teach the same thing. When I showed up for in-line skating classes, we spent the first hour learning how to stop. Fine by me. I comprehended the *theory* of the heel brake. My problem was that even when I was standing still, my skates wanted to move out from under me.

Lonny, the instructor, showed me how to find my center. "Stand with your feet parallel and you won't roll." I continued to slide slowly across the parking lot. "Try it again. Make your feet parallel."

"They *are* parallel," I said.

"They're not, babe. Look down."

There were my feet, splayed out like a duck's. When I made them really parallel, it felt as if my knees were pointed in.

Lonny demonstrated. "Now, with your feet parallel and your arms held out to the sides, imagine the center of your body. It'll be right around your waist at first. Now, bring it down. Bring your center down to your belly. Feel it? Feel that center moving down?"

Wow, I stopped rolling and I felt good. Lonny gave me a high-five. "Practice that all week," he said. "Once you find your center, you are balanced. You can do anything!"

Finding your center also works for public speaking, and the way to center yourself for speaking is to *prepare:*

- Prepare your presentation in every detail.
- Rehearse it by yourself.
- Do a dry run in front of your peers (or have it videotaped).
- Get feedback on your performance.
- Rehearse some more.
- Memorize your three opening lines. Know these lines so well, you will say them even if you're awakened at three A.M. by pounding on the door and voices shouting, "Open up or we'll shoot!"

It's also a good idea to prepare your own introduction and give it to the emcee ahead of time. Nothing throws you off center more than being surprised by what's said to introduce you. At best, the emcee could say you are extremely funny: "Be prepared to laugh!" This is sure to put your audience into a rigid antilaugh mode. At worst, the emcee could say something that embarrasses you or is not true. You can't confront him without sounding negative—just when you most need to sound positive.

> Do a quick-fix tai chi. Rock slowly back and forth from your heels to your toes. Let your arms swing as they will. It's soothing, like sitting in a rocking chair.

Know that you have prepared as well as anyone possibly could. Then stand with your arms out and your feet parallel and find your center. What could it hurt?

## Visualize Your Success

At the end of the first day's skating lesson, Lonny told us to practice the heel brake during the week. "Even if you don't have your own skates, you can practice in your mind. See yourself with your arms out in front, sliding that right foot forward, and then just sitting down. See it clearly and in great detail. Practice that perfect heel brake in your mind."

You can use this same imaging to reduce your speech fears. See yourself walking calmly to the front of the room. Imagine each part of your presentation. Imagine the questions you are asked at the end, and see yourself answering them calmly and competently.

Do it over and over.

By the time you actually get up on stage, you'd think your red alert system would be bored with the whole thing. *Do we have to do this again? We've done this presentation so many times, I think I'll just sleep through this one.* Through repetition, you *may* be able to desensitize your red alert system somewhat, but not entirely. What *will* happen is you'll go on automatic pilot while your body is raging and storming. By the time your brain gets the message that you're not going to be publicly humiliated, it'll settle down and you can enjoy yourself.

## Learn to Shorten the Time You're Scared

Jeffrey, a research chemist, loves to make explosives, and he's a genius at it. He also loves to eat hot peppers—the hotter the better. Working with high-energy propellants for rockets doesn't faze him, but speak in front of a group? He'd rather be gnawed to death by low-IQ rats.

If you're like Jeffrey, look in your phone book or local newspaper for a group called Toastmasters International. They meet usually weekly to offer supportive and specific evaluation of your speaking skills. It starts out easy with a little five-minute story from your life. No one will laugh at you; they'll just help. Other beginners will be there, just as scared as you are.

> Don't worry about getting rid of the butterflies in your stomach. Just get them to fly in formation.
>
> —ESMOND LYONS, Member of Toastmasters International

When I joined Toastmasters, my first five-minute speech took me two weeks to prepare. I had an uneasy stomach for two days before the speech, sheer terror during it, and for fifteen minutes after the speech my hands shook so much I couldn't take notes on the helpful things the evaluator was saying. One thing I remember him saying—although I couldn't write it down—was, "You seemed a little nervous, but believe me you'll get over it."

You also get written evaluations. Mine were very kind. Susan, who was sitting next to me at the speakers table, wrote, "No need to be nervous—you have all the necessary equipment to be a terrific speaker. I don't think your tremors showed much, if at all, from out front."

Some people suggest reducing your nervousness by imagining that the members of the audience are all naked. I discourage this plan, because if you have any sexuality at all, you'll be sneaking peeks instead of focusing on your talk. I recommend imagining them all in old, tattered underwear. Faded boxer shorts frayed at the cuffs. Bra straps pinned with rusty safety pins. You can't be afraid of people that badly dressed.

I've never entirely lost my nervousness before a speech, but the nervous time has gradually shrunk—from a full week, to a day, then to an hour. Now I've shortened it to just those few minutes while I'm being introduced. During those minutes, my eyes water, so I wipe my eyes and clean my glasses. Then I know the worst is over. I stand up, thank my introducer, look out at this kindly group of people sitting there in their tattered underwear, and begin my brilliant presentation.

## Imagine It's Over

When your presentation is over, you can begin to savor it. Why not imagine that pleasure now? I've found that I always give three presentations:

- The presentation I prepare and practice.
- The one I actually present.
- The one I give on the way home from the meeting.

I always like the third one best because I'm now elated but not on edge. I can revise at will and make it perfect. Imagine—now—that delight in giving a great presentation.

Don't forget to visualize the exhilaration you will feel after doing something you were afraid of doing. For my fortieth birthday, my husband gave my son and me a gift certificate for scuba lessons. I did well in the pool, but for our final test, we drove down to Monterey, California. We went down into that cold, dark ocean, where we had to do horrible things like taking off our face masks or detaching our air hoses to share air with a partner. Down there, I gathered a few shells, but as I came back to shore through the surf, survival took over. My hands dropped the shells. Lying flat on my face in the sand, I felt the instructor tap my foot. "Congratulations, you passed." I rose from the sand and did a noisy dance of triumph.

If nothing else, you can look forward to being grateful the audience didn't stone you. After a week of intensive meditations, a Zen Master concluded his talk to a group this way:

> Now we have finished. Everyone stand and we will bow to the Buddha three times to thank him. We thank him, because even if we did not have a great enlightenment, we had a small enlightenment. If we did not have a small enlightenment, at least we didn't get sick. If we got sick, at least we didn't die. So let's thank the Buddha.

## EIGHT PRACTICAL THINGS TO DO JUST BEFORE YOUR TALK

1. Wear suitable but comfortable clothes. Once I gave a talk wearing a too short skirt. It felt great when I was walking or sitting, but up on the high podium, all I could think about was keeping my knees together.
2. Have water on hand where you will sit *before* you speak. Some speakers can cure a dry mouth by taking a sip of water during their presentation. Don't count on it if your hands are shaking up a storm.
3. Repeat after me: "It isn't happening now." This works best when it isn't actually happening, to quell those preview fears. For example, it works well for me when I'm dreading a visit to the dentist. "It isn't happening now."
4. Meditate. Sitting or walking. Remember that walking meditation is not just pacing, although pacing is okay, too.
5. Do raspberries. Blow out through relaxed lips to relax your facial muscles. This exercise is best done in private. A chemical engineer at

a national conference was doing raspberries in the ladies' room just before her presentation, and a woman next to her at the mirror gave her a look. When she went on stage, she was mortified that this same woman was the executive who introduced her.

6.  Rotate your head in a slow circle to relax your neck and throat. It won't take away the tension, but it will make your voice sound less tense.

7.  Breathe in slightly and breathe out strongly in a long hiss. I do this when I'm really terrified—like when I'm approaching the freeway on-ramp. Dorothy Sarnoff in *Never Be Nervous Again* calls this type of breathing the "Sarnoff squeeze." She says it tightens the abdominal muscles surrounding the diaphragm, thereby preventing noradrenaline from forming. I don't know if this is physically true, but it works for me.

8.  While you're waiting to speak, get all your fidgeting done. Straighten your tie or tuck in your blouse, push your glasses up on your nose, scratch where you need to scratch. Then stand up and don't do it anymore.

## FOUR THINGS TO REMEMBER DURING YOUR TALK

1.  Remember to smile. Just smile. You may look simple, but it's hard to feel really bad while you're smiling.

2.  Remember that the audience wants you to succeed. They came to hear you and they are rooting for you.

3.  Remember that your job is to interest and entertain the audience. Don't try to "be funny." A small child can make us laugh with a silly thing because the child is doing it unself-consciously. When an older child or an adult tries the same thing, it's not funny.

4.  Remember to avoid looking at the person sleeping in the third row. It will demoralize you. There's one in every audience. I think they come to meetings just to get over jet lag. Look at the people who are leaning forward in their chairs. Look at the people who appear interested. If they are all asleep, shut up and go home.

# HOW TO FUNCTION SUCCESSFULLY WHILE DOING THE THING SOME PEOPLE FEAR MORE THAN DEATH

Practice the nonaction of *Wu Wei,* the "sitting quietly, doing nothing" way of working through speech fright.

- Know it's okay to be nervous. Recognize that burst of adrenaline and use it to give your talk natural energy.
- Observe what you're feeling without judging it. Say, *Look at that tremor. I'm starting to sweat. Goodness, I didn't know my heart could beat this fast.*
- Maximize your chances for composure by being fully prepared.
- Visualize your successful presentation as you prepare it.
- Keep reducing the time you need to be nervous. With practice, you can get it down to a couple of minutes.
- Think about how good you will feel when it's over.

# Right Speech

## HOW TO GIVE THE SWEET PITCH

●

*It usually takes more than three weeks to prepare a good impromptu speech.*
—MARK TWAIN

●

One element of Buddhist spiritual practice is called "right speech." Buddha taught that right speech should be timely, truthful, kind, and helpful. This guidance is also useful in planning your presentation. In chapter 3, I assigned you a koan—Who is my reader?—and asked you to meditate on it constantly as you write a proposal. Now I'm giving you a new koan:

Who is my audience?

If you meditate on this koan constantly as you plan a presentation, your talk will be well on its way to being timely, truthful, kind, and helpful to your audience. That's known as "the sweet pitch."

We are often told to present our ideas simply, but not how to do it. I remember a presentation by a physicist and engineer, describing his work on using global positioning systems (GPS) to replace radar on guided interceptor missiles. The pleasing thing about his presentation was how simply he described this complex high technology. He could have given us the volume and weight of the launched missile—in metric units, of course. Instead, he said:

We shot off a missile about the size of a Volkswagen from Vandenberg Air Force Base in California and hit it with a missile fired away across the Pacific Ocean off Kwajalein. Now, this was like trying to hit a bullet with a bullet.

Immediately, we understood how hard this task was and were eager to hear how he'd done it. Speaking simply and directly about a complex subject is obviously possible. Why don't we all do it?

The single secret of the sweet pitch is to keep it simple. Say only what needs to be said in that setting and for that particular audience. To find this simplicity and to develop the sweet pitch, you need to begin by answering the following questions:

- Why am I making this presentation?
- What's new about my idea?
- How can I make it compelling to this audience?
- How can I make even complex ideas clear to the listeners?
- How long should I talk?

Let's take these questions one at a time.

## WHY AM I MAKING THIS PRESENTATION?

A presentation can have four purposes:

- To inform.
- To recommend.
- To direct.
- To entertain.

Here are the questions you need to ask yourself before you plan each type of presentation:

- If you are speaking to inform, ask yourself: What do the listeners want to do? What do they need to know to take that action?
- If you are speaking to recommend an action, ask: What decision do the listeners need to make? What information do they need to make that decision?

- If you are speaking to direct people, ask: What action do I want the listeners to perform? How can I help them perform successfully?
- If your purpose is to entertain, ask: What will amuse this group of people? How can I best entertain them?

The kinds of presentations I'm hearing now in Silicon Valley, however, combine all four of these purposes. The speaker wants to inform the listeners about his or her new idea, recommend that they invest in it, direct them as to the benefits of investing, while keeping them awake by being entertaining. If you're giving this kind of talk, you'll need to answer all the questions given above.

## WHAT'S NEW ABOUT MY IDEA?

You've all heard those speeches. The speaker is well groomed, confident, and uses expressive gestures. The voice is well controlled, the PowerPoint slides are professional, and the speaker knows all the tricks to giving a smooth presentation. But the speaker has nothing new to say.

One way to force yourself to identify what's new about your idea is to work up an "elevator pitch." Imagine finding yourself alone in an elevator with the person who has the authority to buy your idea. You have only a few floors—a minute or two—to present your idea. What you want to give is a pithy summary of your idea that is so clearly presented, even a CEO can remember it. If the CEO doesn't remember it, the deal almost never happens.

Your elevator pitch needs to quickly answer this question: If your idea works, what difference will it make? Here are three examples of elevator pitches that worked for selling new technology at SRI International, a research and innovation company in Silicon Valley.

1. We're working on special multipurpose yarns that can be woven into a bulletproof vest to provide lightweight protection as well as battery power to the soldier or police officer. This vest will combine a new super-strength yarn with long-lasting batteries contained in flexible polymers.
2. We are developing a rapid, cost-effective, drug discovery system that could save the pharmaceutical industry tens of millions of dollars for

each new drug discovered. The system is solid state, massively parallel, and programmable and it can test hundreds of compounds at the same time.

3. Our new idea for protecting e-commerce Web sites from subversion or shutdown is a protection system that distributes lightweight sensors over the whole enterprise. It can look inside even encrypted communications, and it is proactive—automatically finding irregularities before they can harm the Web site.

The elevator pitch also works marvelously in other areas, such as pitching the idea for a movie or a book. Olivia Goldsmith, author of *The First Wives Club*, said that when you pitch an idea to Hollywood producers, you need to be very brief because their memory span is so short. To pitch her novel *Switcheroo*, she told the producers:

A woman who has everything—husband, fine house, children—finds that her husband is having an affair with a woman who is ten years younger, twelve pounds lighter, and much blonder. Except for this, the two women look exactly alike. Instead of dumping this guy, the two women switch places, because every wife wants to be treated like a mistress and every mistress wants to be a wife.

> Cats seem to go on the principle that it doesn't do any harm to ask for what you want.
>
> —JOSEPH WOOD KRUTCH

Chris Peterson used this ingenious elevator pitch to an editor to sell her book, *I Love the Internet, but I Want My Privacy, Too!*

Let me show you how much I can find out about a person with a name very close to yours in just fifteen minutes on the Internet.

Chris found the home phone number, address, and precise directions to this person's home with a map. She also checked the California Bankruptcy Records and found several adverse filings and lawsuits including bankruptcy. She was starting to check the stock ownership records databases when her time was up.

Remember the ideas we brainstormed in chapter 6 to persuade our manager to hold the off-site meeting in Hawaii? Your elevator pitch for that presentation could go something like this:

> I recommend that we rent a large house in a remote area of Kauai or rent the Zen retreat on Maui, where we can have privacy for productive work in a relaxed setting while saving money by getting group discounts on airfare, lodging, and food.

## HOW CAN I MAKE IT COMPELLING TO THIS AUDIENCE?

The elevator pitch is an excellent way to zero in on the core of your new idea, and you can often use it as the opening—or conclusion—to your talk. Now, how can you make the rest of your talk as simple and compelling as the opening? Remember that a presentation needs to be more tightly structured than a written proposal because the listeners can't check the table of contents or reread what they've just heard. You don't want to lose their attention while they try to puzzle out where you're going with this idea. The traditional way is to set up a tight structure of the following elements:

- An **opening** that very briefly sets the stage and tells why you are giving this talk (like the cover and dust jacket of a book).
- A **preview** that tells your audience where you're going (the way a table of contents does).
- The body of your talk, which covers **your main points** in a logical order with examples and details.
- A **closing** that summarizes what you've told them and reinforces your recommendations.

Using that framework, we could sketch out our presentation for the next off-site meeting like this:

- **The opening.** [Our manager] asked me to recommend a site for our next off-site meeting. I've looked over the options for a place that will give us a relaxed setting for productive work at low cost.

- **The preview.** I recommend we hold our meeting in a remote part of Kauai or Maui. Let me tell you why Kauai/Maui offers us the most advantages.
- **My points.** I'll just list them for now:
    1. Conducive to productivity.
    2. Cost control.
    3. Lodging options.
    4. Site advantages.
    5. Low-cost activities.
    6. Optional activities.

    (We've probably got too many points here for a short talk, but we can pare them down or combine them as we start writing.)
- **The close.** I recommend that we rent a large house in a remote area of Kauai or rent the Zen retreat on Maui, where we can have privacy for productive work in a relaxed setting while saving money by getting group discounts on airfare, lodging, and food.

This traditional structure works well, but what if you are competing with other people and their great ideas? How can you be sure to grab your listeners' attention? Curt Carlson, CEO of SRI International, came up with a simple way to structure a presentation to hold the audience's attention and deal with the competition. This structure is called NABC:

| | |
|---|---|
| *N:* | customer-market *needs* |
| *A:* | our compelling *approach* |
| *B:* | customer *benefits* (value = benefits/$) |
| *C:* | worldwide *competition* (or *alternatives*) |

In stimulating scientists and engineers to sell their ideas, Carlson gives this example:

| | |
|---|---|
| *Need:* | I need two slices of toast each morning when I am still drowsy. |
| *Approach:* | A two-slice, 120-volt electric toaster. |
| *Benefits:* | I get uniform toast at reasonable cost. It's safe and fast and uses a standard outlet. |

| | |
|---|---|
| *Competition:* | The blowtorch. The disadvantages are it toasts unevenly, it might blow up, and it needs gas refills. |

Researchers at SRI prepare for their first meeting with potential investors in several steps. They first pull together their best presentation of the new technology, then pitch it to colleagues—some are experts in their field, some not. Often, after the first pitch, even the experts say, "I don't get it. I don't understand what you're selling." The presenters go back and tighten and revise, then pitch it again. This pitching practice may go through six or eight revisions until the presenters have honed their pitch and can deliver it with vigor and conviction—until even the nonexperts say, "Ah, I get it."

We can easily apply this NABC structure to our presentation about the off-site meeting in Hawaii:

| | |
|---|---|
| *Need:* | A place that will give us a relaxed setting for productive work at low cost. |
| *Approach:* | Hold our meeting in a remote part of Kauai or Maui. Get group discounts. |
| *Benefits:* | Conducive to productivity, cost control, site advantages, low-cost activities. |
| *Competition:* | Local hotel: Saves airfare, but room rates are high. Too near distractions of the office and home needs. |
| | New York or Paris: Expensive. Group will be splintered by attractions of the city. |
| | Overalls, Georgia: Cheap, but hot and boring. |

You now have a good framework for your talk. As you start developing your slides, you'll refine this structure. You may delete some ideas and add others, but at least you have the structure that will keep your listeners on track.

## HOW CAN I MAKE EVEN COMPLEX IDEAS CLEAR TO THE LISTENERS?

Most speakers use humor in their opening remarks to put the audience—and themselves—at ease. But humor is also an excellent way to clarify complex subjects. You can use humorous analogies to see if your audience understands what you're saying. Their laughter gives you instant feedback.

For example, the creator of the second elevator pitch given above was presenting his new, cost-effective method for very rapidly discovering new drugs. The innovation of this technology was the computer manipulation of tens of thousands of levitated beads (the possible new drugs) over microarrays of plates containing the testing compounds. He gave this example to show how his method was different from existing techniques:

> Suppose you have a classroom of kids who are going to have cookies and milk in the afternoon. The kids get to choose from three kinds of milk: plain milk, chocolate milk, and strawberry milk. Once the kids have chosen, how do you deliver the milk? One way is to use robots to deliver the chosen milk to each kid. That's the current method used to screen drugs in the wet lab. Or you could construct a system of pipes under the tables to deliver the milk. That's microfluidics, also used today. A third way would be to move the kids around, allowing them to dunk their cookies into the type of milk they like. That's our new method—diamagnetic levitation.

Of course, this wasn't just humor, but a very good analogy, presented in a simple, lighthearted way. But when the audience laughed, the speaker knew immediately that they understood how his method was different.

## HOW LONG SHOULD I TALK?

How long you should talk depends on the answer to your assigned question: Who is my audience? Many audiences will limit your time. For example:

- If you've caught your potential buyer in an elevator, you can talk for only two or three minutes.
- If your audience is an editor or agent at a writers conference, you must grab your target in five minutes, although the Maui Writers Conference will let you buy fifteen minutes.

- If your audience is there for an oral defense of your proposal, they'll give you an hour or two, but you need to leave plenty of that time for their questions.
- If your audience is a group of venture capitalists, you'll be lucky to get ten minutes without interruptions.

Venture capitalists can be the toughest audience of all. A former investment banker told me that investors are usually impatient to hear the crux of the idea. They often interrupt to ask questions, and they usually have other deals on their minds. The investment banker said, "They not only receive calls on their cell phones during a presentation; they *make* calls."

For a recent presentation to venture capitalists, each speaker was allowed only ten minutes. For such a short talk, slides needed to be edited down and simplified. Graphics were used to save words. Here's how sparsely the nine slides were allocated for each ten-minute presentation:

1 slide for the opening (name of the presentation and presenter's name).
1 slide for the elevator pitch.
2 slides for the need (key business trends and customer needs).
2 slides for the approach (how it works).
1 slide for benefits to the customer.
1 slide for the competition (and why our idea is better).
1 slide for status, intellectual property, and next steps.

The objective here was to capture and hold the investors' attention, not to explain everything in detail. If you've captured your audience's attention and they ask to hear more, you can have a binder of sixty slides as backup. But don't pull them out unless the customer asks for more. If you're lucky enough to be asked back for a second meeting, you can give all the details then.

Jack, a technical illustrator, sold encyclopedias door to door when he was nineteen. This is the most important lesson he learned:

Don't talk past the close. You've got their interest, and they're eager to buy. Now stop talking. Hand them the contract and a pen.

When I pitched the idea for this book at a writers conference, I had five minutes to sell my idea to a publisher. I made it past my first three carefully planned sentences, and the publisher seemed interested. He leaned forward when I said it was a short, funny, how-to book for people trying to sell all kinds of proposals. I seemed hear him say, "I don't think there *are* any other funny books about proposals." I saw his eyes dilate when I said I'd been a technical writer and editor for twenty-five years. Then I started to talk about the competition. I *think* he said, "I'd like to see your proposal." I plunged desperately into my routine about the possible markets for the book. He finally had to say the psychiatrist's words "Well, I think our time is up." I left him a one-page summary and slipped away as he turned to the next writer.

Don't talk past the close.

## EXERCISES FOR PLANNING THE SWEET PITCH

To incorporate the Buddhist concept of right speech, your presentation needs to be timely, truthful, kind, and helpful to your audience. One exercise for reaching that goal is to meditate on this question: Who is my audience? Here are some other exercises for planning your presentation.

**Exercise 1:** State the core of your idea in one to three sentences. Imagine the CEO in the elevator or your best friend on a busy street corner. Write the words to complete this sentence: My new idea for _____ is to _____. Or: My new way to solve the problem of _____ is to _____.

**Exercise 2:** Look at your idea now and write out the needs, approach, benefits, and competition statements.
Keep working on the benefits until they're not just the *features* of your idea, but the *benefits* or advantages to the user. Look at the toaster example again. Having the capacity for two slices and using 120 volts are features of the idea, not the benefits. For other examples, go back to chapter 4, "What Does Your Client Want to Buy?"

**Exercise 3:** Write one paragraph on what's new about your idea. How is it different from and better than previous ideas? If it is successful, what difference will it make in the world?

**Exercise 4:** Write down three ways you will know when your listener is interested in your idea. How will you know when to stop talking? Be very specific.

# The Speaker from Hell

## 17

As a perceptive reader, you'll quickly notice there's no Zen in this chapter. That's because there's no concept of hell in Zen. Like most editors, however, I'm obsessive about being consistent—even though Zen is not at all consistent—so let me tell you one Zen story.

A monk was chased by a tiger off the edge of a cliff. The monk grabbed on to a vine that had grown over the edge. Below him was the long drop to sure death, and above him was the menacing tiger. As the monk was swinging in the air, he noticed a mouse gnawing at the vine above him. He also noticed a wild strawberry growing out of the cliff. He picked the strawberry and ate it, saying, "This strawberry is delicious."

I think this story is supposed to show us how to live in the moment, to savor each part of life as it is. The story could also mean that we can find some good even in the middle of terrible times. As you read this chapter about the worst mistakes speakers make, try to turn these mistakes around to find the good things speakers can do to keep the interest of the audience.

## RECOGNIZING THE SPEAKER FROM HELL

From the speaker's first words, you know you're going to hate this presentation: "I hope no one minds, but I'm changing the topic a bit from the topic announced in the program." Or worse, "Rather than present the topic announced in the program, how would it be if I just answered questions from the audience?" When you hear these opening statements, check quickly to see how close you are to the end of a row or the back of the room. Better yet, slip out now. You won't be sorry. The presenter is going to go on forever, never getting to the topic you came to hear. How can we be so sure? Because experienced audiences know how to translate statements made by the speaker from hell.

| WHAT THE SPEAKER SAYS | WHAT THE AUDIENCE UNDERSTANDS |
| --- | --- |
| "I'm changing the topic a bit from the topic announced in the program." | I don't care what you came here to hear. I'm going to talk about what interests me. |
| "Rather than talk on the topic announced in the program, how would it be if I just answered questions from the audience?" | I'm too lazy to prepare a presentation. You do it for me. |
| "I realize I have too many slides for twenty minutes, so I'll just run through them quickly." | I'm going to cover every single point if it takes all summer. |
| "I know you can't see these numbers on the screen, so I'll just summarize them for you." | I couldn't be bothered to make slides you could actually see. |
| "I'll ask you to hold your questions until the end." | I don't want to be interrupted. If you will simply listen to all I have to say, you couldn't possibly have any questions unless you are stupid. |
| "Those who can't hear me might want to move to the front of the room." | I am so important, you should be willing to sit leaning forward, straining to hear every word I say. |
| "Please excuse me for being a bit disorganized here." | I didn't bother to practice this speech because you are such an unimportant audience. |

Sometimes you can't tell right away how bad it's going to be. Let me take you through an actual presentation from hell, told to me by a friend I shall call Lulu. On the advice of my editor, who worries about libel suits, I have also disguised the topic, the speaker, and the setting. So don't send me e-mail saying you were at this meeting. Here's Lulu's description of the presentation she had to sit through.

We arrive at the Farmers Coop, eager to hear a presentation on how to sell rutabagas to third world countries. The professor of agriculture looks intelligent and is well dressed. He speaks clearly and seems at ease in front of the audience of farmers who are looking for ways to market their surplus crops.

After several slides, it becomes apparent that the speaker has wandered off into the scientific details of his plan for increasing the per-acre yield of vegetables. We who grow rutabagas have no need for increased

> Half the world is composed of people who have something to say and can't, and the other half who have nothing to say and keep saying it.
>
> —ROBERT FROST

yields. We have rutabagas rotting in the ground now for lack of markets. The speaker has a two-inch-thick, three-ring binder full of slides. *Bad sign.* But I have chosen a seat in the middle of a long row. There's no way to escape.

Ten minutes into the presentation, I notice two people with their eyelids drooping. One woman sits with her legs and arms crossed, frowning at the speaker. As a polite member of the audience, I try to keep a look of interest on my face but finally decide it doesn't matter because the speaker stands with his back to us most of the time. He is speaking to his slides—apparently the most interested members of the audience. I wonder if he could be marketed as a soporific for insomniacs.

The speaker announces he will now talk about what to do with excess yields. Yes! *This is what we came for.* But instead of rutabagas, he is now talking, it seems, about his plan for dealing with the excess large zucchini produced in New Hampshire. As if we weren't now using those big guys for doorstops. All his plans are delivered in complex scientific terms. Now, we're farmers, and we know a lot about agricultural science, but what do transgenic, biofunctional, monoclonal antibodies have to do with zucchini? As near as I can figure, he is recommending injecting bacteria into large zucchini, then compressing them to use as filler for roadbeds.

After forty minutes the speaker says, "Now, before I go on to talk about frambled thrushmuggers and their biomorphic phase transformations, does anyone have any questions?" He's going to go on? He says, "I see some sleepy eyes in the audience. Doesn't anyone want to ask a controversial question?" He knows we're dying here. He knows! But he's going to keep on.

Someone mumbles a question from the front of the room. The speaker gives a four-minute answer to a question we have not heard. I begin trying to estimate the number of slides left in the stack. At one to two minutes each, that's—my God, that's forever.

We finally hear those blessed words, "And in summary . . ." *Thank you, Jesus.* People begin to stir and shift in their seats, like passengers after a ten-hour transoceanic flight. I notice he still has half an inch of slides left. *How long, Lord, how long?*

To avoid being the speaker from hell, you can simply reverse these wrongs, as we will explore below.

---

**Where Did This Speaker Go Wrong?**

* He spoke about what he wanted to say rather than what the audience wanted to hear.
* He spoke in a language they couldn't understand.
* He didn't respect his audience's needs.
* He didn't know when to stop.

---

## GIVE THEM WHAT THEY CAME FOR

You made a commitment to talk on this subject, so do it. If you're sick to death of talking about rutabaga surplus, get over it. If you aren't yet sure of your topic when it's time for the program to be printed, give them a vague, evasive title. "Facing the New Millennium" is popular just about now.

If you are famous or gorgeous and they are coming simply because *you* are talking, you can talk about anything. They won't care. Check first with someone neutral—someone who doesn't love you and doesn't owe you money—to be sure you are truly in this category.

## KNOW YOUR AUDIENCE'S LANGUAGE

Know your audience: Why are they there, and what type of language will they understand? Every field has its own jargon, but not all jargon will be understood by your listeners. If you don't know *their* jargon, don't try to speak it. Keep it simple and direct.

In the seventies, scientists were trying to find a way to turn coal into a liquid so it could be pumped through pipelines rather than hauled in trucks and dumped in messy piles. I was editing then for Dr. Frank Mayo at Stanford Research Institute. The junior chemists in Dr. Mayo's group wrote up the experimental procedures in quarterly reports:

> Our second approach to breaking down the molecular structure of coal consisted of the addition of sodium hypochlorite to a borosilicate beaker containing 2 mL of anthracite No. 6.

In a summary of the work, presented at a meeting of the CEOs of big chemical companies, Dr. Mayo simply said:

> We then tried pouring Clorox over coal in Pyrex beakers.

Within the language of every field, there are levels of understanding that lead down to impenetrability. Po Bronson, in *The Nudist on the Late Shift and Other True Tales of Silicon Valley*, gives the following conversation between George (a futurist) and Steve (CEO of a company that produces Internet servers and routers), who "go through a sort of cascade of language syntax, negotiating like two modems, trying to find the most efficient level of conversation they can hold":

> GEORGE: Hi, nice to meet you. Hey, that's a sweet access router over there. Wow, both Ethernet and asynchronous ports?
>
> STEVE: Yeah, check this baby out—the Ethernet port has AUI, BNC, and RJ-45 connectors.
>
> GEORGE: So for the packet filtering you went with TCP, UDP, and ICMP.
>
> STEVE: Of course. To support dial-up SLIP and PPP.
>
> GEORGE: Set user User__Name ifilter Filter__Name.
>
> STEVE: Set filter s1.out 8 permit 192.9.200.2/32 0.0.0.0/0 tcp src eq 20.
>
> GEORGE: 00101101110001011100100l 1101000010101010001111001.
>
> STEVE: . .. .. . . . . . . ... .. .. ... .. .. . . . . . .. ..
>
> GEORGE: Really? Wait, you lost me there.

Other fields besides the computer industry have developed languages that are incomprehensible to outsiders. Here's a difficult quiz. See if you can match the speakers of these quotes with their occupations. Only four out of ten people I gave this quiz to were able to get them all right. The answers are at the end of this chapter.

| THE SPEAKER'S JARGON | THE SPEAKER'S OCCUPATION |
|---|---|
| 1. I'd say it has an exquisite nose and great legs. | a. Roof framing carpenter |
| 2. He earned out the advance in only three months. | b. Doctor |
| 3. "It use to be a hair band, but now they do postmetal funk with a ska kick." | c. Book editor/publisher |
| 4. Their burn rate is $12 million a year, but with that short a runway, they'll need an exit strategy. | d. Kindergarten teacher |
| 5. Our daily schedule facilitates both large and small muscular activity development. | e. Venture capitalist |
| 6. We'll ambulate him after the extubation in the morning. | f. Record producer |
| 7. It's a bastard valley, but it still hits the ridge at the true hip. | g. Wine taster |

(*Clue:* The third speaker is a character in *Be Cool* by Elmore Leonard.)

Sometimes the phrases we use are understandable, but they are used in the wrong situation. For example, the phrases "Hazardous conditions may apply here" and "Utilize caution" are both clear, but they don't fit if gunshots are zinging all around you.

Using the wrong *level* of language can also stifle communication. Lulu (again) and her husband, Horvé, were having some "relationship difficulties," so they made an appointment with a sex therapist. They arrived ready to talk about their sex life but immediately ran into a vocabulary roadblock. Whenever they talked naturally about what was happening to them in bed, the therapist said, "What I hear you saying is . . ." and then rephrased it all into medical and anatomical terms. "We couldn't get past the language barrier," said Lulu. "The therapist kept talking about sexual intercourse. I tried to talk about making love. And Horvé persisted in talking about—well, screwing."

## RESPECT YOUR AUDIENCE'S NEEDS

Put yourself in the place of the audience. For example, don't ask, "Can everyone hear me?" No one person can answer that question. (My third-grade teacher always asked us, "Is everyone finished?" How could we know?) It's also ridiculous to ask those who cannot hear you to hold up their hands. A better plan is to point to one particular person in the very back of the room, "Can *you* hear me clearly back there?" If he doesn't answer, he can't.

Always repeat the questions from the audience before you answer them. Repeating the question not only ensures that your audience has heard the question, it gives *you* time to frame your answer. Repeating the questions is even more important when your talk is being recorded. One speaker, who was repeatedly reminded to repeat the questions, snarled, "Why don't you all just speak up?" It was useless to remind him that people in the next room were watching on a video hookup. All they heard were vague answers to unknown questions.

Sometimes a question is so long and rambling, neither you nor the audience is sure just what is being asked. Here, especially, you need to reframe the question. Be courteous to these questioners, but don't let them give a speech. Try to interrupt gently and say, "I believe your question is . . ."

## STOP WHEN YOUR TIME IS UP

Running over the time allotted you is rude to the next speaker and makes the audience cranky. If it's too long when you rehearse it, it's still going to be too long when you present it. Take out some words.

If you have thirty slides for a twenty-minute talk, you're already in trouble. Take out some slides. One slide for each minute is a rough guide, but only if your slides are very pithy (three or four lines only). For a ten-minute talk, limit yourself to nine slides, *including* the one that just gives your name and the title of your talk. For an hour's presentation, don't bring more than forty-five slides.

●

## TIPS FOR AVOIDING BEING THE SPEAKER FROM HELL

It boils down to courtesy to your listeners. Here are some ways to be tough with yourself so you think about the needs of your audience:

- Give them what they came for. You made a commitment to talk on this subject, so do it.
- Use jargon only if you're positive they will understand you. Even then, tailor it to your audience, the occasion, and the setting.
- Respect your audience by making sure they can hear you and by repeating the questions.
- Stop talking when your time is up.
- Remember always that you are up there at their pleasure. Do you want to be invited back?

## Answers to Jargon Quiz

1, g; 2, c; 3, f; 4, e; 5, d; 6, b; 7, a.

# Enlightenment

## MEETING WITH YOUR CLIENT

## 18

If you flinch at the idea of yet another meeting in your busy schedule, you may enjoy this story about a modern Japanese emperor whose
day was "so tightly scheduled that it would make a stone wall seem
open by comparison," as told by Benjamin Hoff in *The Tao of Pooh:*

> In the middle of a particularly busy day, the emperor was driven
> to a meeting hall for an appointment of some kind. But when
> he arrived, there was no one there. The emperor walked into the
> middle of the great hall, stood silently for a moment, then bowed
> to the empty space. He turned to his assistants, a large smile on his
> face. "We must schedule more appointments like this," he told
> them. "I haven't enjoyed myself so much in a long time."

Meetings are something we usually try to avoid because they are
boring and a waste of time. But a meeting with a potential client can be
enlightening, and it is the only way to gain mutual trust. At my company, we often ask our potential clients to come visit us. They like to
come because they get to visit California and then spend the weekend
in San Francisco. We like it because we get to control the meeting and
show them all our best toys.

When you are planning a meeting with a potential client, your presentation will be one of the high points. But your presentation is only
one of many details to consider. Planning for a client's visit requires
great care in choosing the setting, rehearsing your best speakers,
scheduling the pace of the day, providing a light lunch, and getting
dinner reservations at that upscale French restaurant. These details are
important, but don't get so caught up in them that you forget the real

goals of the meeting: to gain trust, to determine your client's needs, and to generate a cooperative atmosphere for future interactions.

## THE FIRST MEETING

Your goals for the first meeting with potential clients should be very simple:

- Meet them.
- Get to know and trust them.
- Get them to trust you.

Trust may not develop in the first meeting. In fact, first meetings can be misleading. In my first meeting with a literary agent at a writers conference, I misjudged him completely. Most of the agents at the conference let you pitch your book for a full five minutes before they said a few words and moved on to the next writer. But this agent talked about his company for the full twenty-minute session. Because I wanted to talk about *my* book, I decided he was an egocentric jerk.

That night was the presentation of contest prizes, and a short nonfiction piece I'd entered won honorable mention. In an auditorium holding five hundred people, I stepped onto the stage just as they read the title of my article—"Zen and the Art of Proposal Editing"—and this five-hundred-voice roar of a laugh came at me across the footlights.

During a break, the same talkative agent I'd listened to that morning asked me if I'd thought of expanding my nonfiction article into something larger.

"Something larger?"

"I think it could be a good book," he said.

"A book?"

"Yes, a short book. Maybe a hundred and fifty pages."

"A hundred and fifty pages?" *My goodness,* I thought. *I finally got an agent to ask me about my project and all I can do is echo what he's saying.*

As he kept talking, I began to see I *could* write the book. I'd been collecting the material for twenty years. I began adding ideas, and we stood there nodding and laughing and planning the book. I began to see that I was the egocentric jerk. This agent was a man of keen perception and exquisite literary taste.

At your first meeting with a client, you should spend most of your time listening, not talking. After your (short!) presentation, listen carefully to the client's questions. After you answer each question, take the opportunity to ask the client a question. Keep listening until you are sure you fully understand your client's point of view.

## GAINING A CLIENT'S TRUST

In winning contracts, writing the proposal is not the first thing you do. Mohsen, an engineer who has been extremely successful in winning big international contracts, says that the first thing to do is to gain the client's trust.

> You meet with them a lot. Talk on the phone a lot. Mostly, you listen to them. You show you understand their needs. Then you listen some more. Finally, they open up and tell you their *most pressing need*. Writing the proposal is the last step in sealing that trust.

The proposal should be something the client is waiting for, something the client has helped plan. Talk to your clients about how you can help them solve their problems. Get to know their needs. Then, if you can, get them to help you write the proposal. Gary, a training specialist who parlayed a single phone call to our inquiry line into a ten-year, multimillion-dollar contract, says:

> The ideal proposal is one that the client is waiting for eagerly. The client already knows what's going to be in it because you've discussed the ideas together many times. Now you want to make the proposal a big event they are looking forward to seeing.

When clients trust you and feel you truly understand their problems, they'll be receptive to your proposal. You may feel you've already won the contract, and maybe you have. But you are honor-bound to produce a good proposal. At this stage, a good proposal won't be the factor that wins you the contract, but a bad proposal can lose it for you.

I once asked a proposal leader, "If we're so sure we're going to win this proposal, why are we working so hard on it?"

"We've already convinced the client to buy," he said. "What we're doing now is confirming their good judgment."

## REGAINING A CLIENT'S TRUST

Once you gain a client's trust, be careful not to do anything that could lose that trust. Getting a client back on your side is much harder than getting the client in the first place.

Rob, a research chemist, was handed a tough assignment: Get this client back in our good favor. A previous employee had made this client so angry, he'd vowed he'd never give Rob's company another contract. Never mind what the other employee had done. He was gone from the company now, and Rob's manager wanted this client back. Rob wrote the client and left messages but got no answers. He had other people call to set up appointments. No answers. Finally he got the most persuasive person in his Washington office to keep calling, keep being pleasantly persistent, until after three months the client finally agreed to a short meeting. But it had to be at ten o'clock the next morning.

Rob flew from California to Washington on the red-eye and appeared in the client's doorway at precisely 9:59, straightening his tie and smiling pleasantly. The client looked up from his desk and snarled, "You have five minutes. Don't bother to sit down."

Rob began briskly laying out all the benefits to this client of the work he could do for them. At precisely five minutes, Rob was in the middle of saying, "So, the advanced chemistry we've developed could be great for your—"

"Time's up. Go away."

Anyone else would have given up, but Rob knew this client controlled a big budget for just his kind of work. He kept writing, kept calling, until six months later he got another meeting. This time, when Rob appeared in the doorway, the client said, "Ten minutes. Talk and get out." *Hey*, thought Rob, *that's a 100 percent improvement.*

It took two years, but he won the client back. The support of this client allowed Rob to develop his chemistry into an advanced rocket fuel that was more powerful than anything the client had and also didn't pollute the environment. Seven contracts, several million dollars, and two patents later, the client was happy and Rob was a program manager. Rob had turned an angry client into one of our strongest supporters.

You *can* win back a client's trust, but it's hard work. Keeping that client's trust should be your prime objective.

## KEEPING THEIR TRUST

In a presentation on how to convert one-time leads into repeat clients, Mohsen, an engineer, compared what a good waiter does for restaurant customers with what a good program manager needs to do to keep clients coming back for more contracts. Both succeed in gaining customer satisfaction.

| GOOD WAITER | GOOD PROGRAM MANAGER |
|---|---|
| Sizes up: "Celebrating an occasion or just hungry?" | Evaluates client's needs. |
| Doesn't push the "special" if they already know what they want. | Listens more than talks. |
| Helps them make selections from the menu. | Helps client write the Statement of Work. |
| Relies on rapport with a team that includes the chef, busboys, and wine steward to satisfy customer's needs. | Relies on rapport with a team of professionals and support people to satisfy client's needs. |
| Pays timely attention without being intrusive. | Stays tuned to changes in client's current most pressing need. |
| Sweetens the occasion with a free dessert wine. | Delivers more than promised. |
| Cultivates customers so they'll come back and bring their friends. | Gets follow-on projects and referrals. |

Keeping your current clients happy takes much less energy than cultivating the trust of new clients or winning back unhappy clients. George Abrahamson, my manager for fifteen years, had a formula:

Always give your clients more than they paid for. But at the beginning, promise them as little as possible.

## CLOSING THE MEETING

The part of planning for a potential client's visit that's often neglected is how to close the meeting. You know you're not going to close the deal at this first meeting, but how do you ensure that the meeting will lead to the important next steps?

At one of our workshops on client-centered marketing, Jon Clemens, now president and CEO of Sharp Laboratories of America, Inc., gave an excellent presentation entitled "Closing the Meeting." Clemens said that the close is the single most important part of the meeting:

A poor close can waste the entire day.

The purpose of this closing is to determine the potential client's state of mind toward your company. You want to generate an atmosphere of future cooperation and to set the stage for more interactions. You also want to prepare this client for your follow-up. Clemens recommended the following steps.

### Hold a Summary Session

Set aside a specific time at the end of the meeting for a summary session. A person from your company should take charge of this summary, but you want to limit the number of people from your company to as few as possible. You want an honest appraisal of what the visitors think, and it's easier to pry out negative perceptions with fewer people from your company present.

### Get Feedback

Ask the visitors, "What are your impressions of what you saw and heard today?" Don't let them get by with general answers. *Ask specifically about each segment or each presentation.* Take the time to correct any misunderstandings. If you're leading the summary session, have someone take careful notes for feedback later. On a flipchart or whiteboard, list all open issues or open questions. Check with the visitors to be sure you have all the issues.

*Schedule Next Actions*

If there are obvious next actions, list them. Also list a specific person to be responsible for getting it done. Agree on an estimated time to complete these actions. From the open issues and questions, select those that should be answered first. Assign a specific person the responsibility. Agree on an estimated time to complete.

An important step here is to make sure that some of the actions are assigned to the visitors.

*Follow Up*

After the visit, write a follow-up letter to the visitors. Include the list of open issues and questions, the action items, the responsible person, and the estimated completion date. Make sure you and the people at your company complete your action items. Then call and tell the visitors the results of your actions. Call the visitors again after they should have completed their action items (give them an extra week).

Keep calling your visitors. Make up an excuse to call if you need to. Just keep calling as long as communicating is successful. Stop calling when it's no longer successful. Don't keep badgering them. Don't fade away, though; cut it off clean. You can invite them back when they have other interests.

Following these steps will make sure you get as much out of the meeting as possible. Even if nothing tangible is immediately forthcoming, you have taken the first step with a potential client and left them with a good feeling about your company. Next visit, who knows?

## TIPS FOR GAINING YOUR CLIENT'S TRUST

Meeting a client in person is very much like a blind date. Only rarely will you fall in love at first sight. You may even hate each other at first. It can also be the first date of many and lead to a lasting relationship.

Here are some reminders to help you survive the first meeting:

- Plan the meeting carefully to meet your date's needs, not your own.
- Don't expect a contract (or a marriage proposal) on the first date.
- At the end of the date, say thank you and try to find out if they also had a good time.
- Call or send a note (or flowers) the next day.
- Keep calling until you get another date.
- If they tell you to get lost, wait until next year and try again.

# LETTING GO

## It'll Never Be Perfect

# Staying on the Wheel of Life

## 19

GETTING IT THERE ON TIME

You've worked hard on your proposal. You planned it around the needs of your client. You reviewed it and refined it. You cleaned it up and let an editor find the weak spots. And you cleaned it up again. Now, take a deep breath and let it go. It's your baby, but it has to grow up.

Here's a story from Okakura's *The Book of Tea:*

> Rikyu was watching his son Sho-an as he swept and watered the garden path. "Not clean enough," said Rikyu. After a weary hour, his son returned. "Father, there is nothing more to be done. The steps have been washed for the third time, the stone lanterns and trees are well sprinkled with water, moss and lichens are shining with a fresh verdure; not a twig, not a leaf have I left on the ground." "Young fool," chided the teamaster. "That is not the way a garden path should be swept." Saying this, Rikyu stepped into the garden, shook a tree, and scattered over the garden gold and crimson leaves, scraps of the brocade of autumn. What Rikyu demanded was not cleanliness alone, but the beautiful and the natural also.

Your proposal will never be perfect, but perhaps it doesn't need to be perfect. Maybe a few gold and crimson leaves scattered over the path will make it more beautiful and natural.

## SCHEDULE THE TIME TO STOP REFINING

A crucial step in getting your proposal there on time is to stop writing it. As the instructor said during exam time, "Pencils down." Schedule the time when you'll stop revising and refining. Then stop. Unless you stop fussing over it, it won't matter how good your proposal is, because no one is going to read it.

You may need someone to rip the proposal out of your hands. A proposal coordinator, Lisa, had a gentler method for one proposal writer who just couldn't let go. The writer wanted to make "just one more pass" through the proposal. Lisa knew that if he found any errors, there wouldn't be time to make the corrections and still get the proposal out on time. However, she set him up with a copy of the proposal in a quiet room way up the hall, then came back and said to the proposal production team, "Now. Let's get this puppy out the door."

Take heed: If *you* can't let the proposal go, your production staff may just have to do it for you.

## "ON TIME" IS NOT NEGOTIABLE

"We brought it in on time and under budget." That's what you look forward to saying about the project once it's done. But first, it's what you need to do now with the proposal.

"On time" for proposals to the government means the proposal must be in the agency's office, for example, at precisely 1400 hours eastern standard time on 15 November 2000. "Under budget" means it cannot be more than, say, thirty pages, single-spaced (no more than six lines per inch), twelve-point font, and an average of fifteen characters per inch. Foldouts count as two pages.

Many government RFPs are this exacting, and now they've added a new wrinkle. They want you to send the proposal by e-mail or on disk, and they limit the electronic space. A request for applications from NASA's Institute for Advanced Concepts limited the hard copy of the proposal to twelve pages, then said, "The technical proposal converted to PDF format shall not exceed 300 KB in size." An RFP from the U.S. Army gave a twenty-page limit, wanted it submitted by e-mail, but warned that the file could not be larger than 15,000 KB.

Commercial clients may not give any page or electronic limits, but "on time" means if they don't receive it by Tuesday, they won't have time to review it before the board of directors meeting on Friday.

If your proposal is going to Japan, "on time" means yesterday. Japan is fourteen to seventeen hours ahead of the United States (that is, ten to seven hours behind us, but one day ahead because Japan is across the International Date Line), so today is already tomorrow. Therefore, at five P.M. in San Francisco on the day *before* your proposal is due in Japan, it's already ten A.M. the next day in Tokyo.

For international proposals, you may also need to allow time for translation. If you get the proposal to Japan late, the Japanese company will assign the translation to the lowest-level clerks, who will not feel kindly toward you as they stay up all night translating your proposal. Get it there late and you have broken trust—a serious violation of the rules of courtesy in Japan.

## WAR STORIES: WHEN AND HOW TO SEND YOUR PROPOSAL

Plan to send your proposal at least two full days before it's due. This can give you a day for a quick save if the courier misplaces your package. Then build in one *extra* day for solving last minute problems at your office. Ignoring this advice can cause you pain.

Here's an excerpt from a NASA request for applications:

> The deadline for receipt of proposals is absolutely firm and enforced to the minute. Often a few people plan to hand-carry proposals to NASA at the last hour, but miss the deadline because of late airplanes or traffic tie-ups.

These austere words invoke scenes of stress and tragedy. Desperate people dashing through the airport, panicked people shouting at their cabdrivers. People in NASA's front lobby, red-faced and shouting, then realizing it is hopeless and bursting into tears. Perhaps it is to buffer themselves from such embarrassing scenes that the reviewers at NASA now want proposals submitted directly to NASA's Web site.

We once cut a deadline right to the wire because the proposal needed to get only to Oakland—just across the San Francisco Bay Bridge from us. The proposal leader set off in his car with the proposal and ninety minutes to spare. He never made it. Demonstrators surged onto the bridge to demonstrate for open spaces, and the Highway Patrol had to close the bridge. He sat there in traffic, watching his proposal decline to the value of the paper it was written on.

A proposal sent to England was held up by customs for two days. We talked our way out of that one, but it's something we'll allow time for from now on.

Don't be a hero and try to deliver the proposal yourself. Once we had a proposal due in North Carolina the next day, and the proposal author volunteered to carry it on the plane to deliver to our Washington office by eight the next morning. The Washington staff would then put it on a quick hop to North Carolina. We sent him off with the proposal and celebrated with champagne. At nine the next morning (six A.M. Pacific time), the author tore into the Washington office. He had overslept! The last plane to North Carolina had left, and the proposal was lost.

We no longer let people hand-carry a proposal, and we don't celebrate until we have confirmed that the proposal has been *received*. Even with the courier services that guarantee overnight delivery, slipups can happen. When they do, that guarantee means you get a refund on the delivery cost, but you don't get a second chance at winning that million-dollar proposal.

Tad, a proposal coordinator, routinely gets proposals to the right place at the right time. Her company relies on her immensely. Once they put the proposal in her hands, they can relax, knowing the proposal will get there by the deadline—at least 99.99 percent of the time. Tad has some good stories about that 0.01 percent. In the early days of couriers, one courier confirmed that the package (containing two proposals worth a potential $500,000 each) had been delivered on time. Only one small problem. The package had been delivered to Aberdeen, North Dakota, instead of Aberdeen, Maryland.

On another proposal, a late-night courier (let's call it Courier A) picked up from our guard station a package labeled with the air bill for Courier B instead of the one clearly labeled for Courier A. The courier proudly delivered the wrong proposal on time to the puzzled client.

One proposal wasn't ready until late at night—too late for the usual courier service—so we picked a smaller courier that didn't have its own planes but relied on commercial carriers. The next morning, the courier called to say the package *might* be on a flight that had been canceled in Omaha. *Oh, Lord.* Second call: No, it wasn't on that flight. They got it on a second flight, but *that* flight had been delayed. If the pilot could make up the delay time, it *might* get there just in time at 4:00 P.M. The plane landed at 3:48. The truck rushed the proposal to the client, but it arrived there at 4:07. Too late. The doors were locked.

Sometimes even the best couriers have odd reasons for not delivering on time. We recently sent three packages to the identical address at the Office of Naval Research, except that each package was addressed to a different person. Only one package was delivered on time. The second was delayed two hours because the "Recipient was not in," and the third was returned because "Business is closed." All within the same two hours.

In the winter, you must assume that the weather will delay your proposal. One January our proposal made it through rain, sleet, and snow clear across the country. Then, in Washington, D.C., the truck could not deliver it because ice coated the loading dock. By the time the ice was cleared, the proposal was five minutes too late.

Sometimes last minute delivery works. We once hired a motorcycle same-day courier to carry a proposal up to Sacramento. When I called the client to tell him how it was arriving, he said, "Boy, I'm going to run down to the mailroom. I gotta see this! You think he'll be wearing chains?"

## TIPS ON GETTING IT THERE ON TIME

Let it go. Accept the serenity of knowing you've done all that could be done. Whether you're handing the proposal to a courier or pushing the final button that submits the proposal to your client's Web site, it's showtime! Here are some reminders:

- Don't keep working toward perfect. Settle for excellent.
- Schedule the time when you'll put your pencils down. Then stop.
- Plan to send your proposal at least two full days before it's due. This can give you a day for a quick save. Then build in one extra day for solving last minute problems.
- Don't expect the courier service to achieve miracles 100 percent of the time.
- Don't celebrate until the courier confirms delivery.

# Getting Beyond

## 20

**HOW TO RECOVER FROM THE PROPOSAL**

●

*When you do something, you should burn yourself completely, like a good bonfire, leaving no trace of yourself.*

—Suzuki

●

When you're working on an important proposal, you develop a special cocoon world. For weeks or months, you devote all your time and thoughts to this project. Then, finally, it's done. It's in the courier's truck, and a big empty space opens up in your life. It's like coming out of a movie in the middle of the afternoon. Whoa, it's still daylight out here. What do I do with the rest of the day—the rest of my life?

## HOW TO BURN WITH ZEAL WITHOUT BURNING YOURSELF OUT

It's easy to get caught in a goal-focused tunnel in the last frantic stages of a proposal. Even with the best planning and the best intentions of staying serene, you can find yourself in the center of a tornado that sweeps away your center, your family, and your life.

Oh, sure, you've promised yourself a vacation as soon as this is over. You'll take your son to Disneyland to make up for missing his music recital. You'll spend a weekend alone with the person who's been so patient through it all. You'll return your mother's calls.

None of that will help you right now. Instead, here are eight quick ways to create a distance between you and the proposal when frenzy threatens.

1. Take one-minute vacations. Sit up straight and do nothing but take three slow breaths. Water a plant. Go to a window and look up at the moon.

2. Get silly. Smile for no reason. Waddle like a duck to the copy machine.

3. Get moving. Pretend you're a conductor leading a great orchestra. Stand up and wave your arms about, bringing the violins and the trumpets and the kettledrums to a great crescendo. As you listen to the applause, let your arms flop and bend over, hanging limp like a rag doll. Go out and run around the building as fast as you can.

4. Have a meditation ready. Before the proposal rush begins, practice this three-finger exercise. First, touch your thumb to your forefinger and imagine in great detail the most serene and beautiful setting—a leafy glade or a white sandy beach. Second, touch your thumb to your middle finder and recall the finest compliment you've ever received. Third, touch your thumb to your ring finger and re-create your greatest achievement. Whether anyone else valued it or not, you are proud you did it. If you practice this exercise slowly and in great detail, then when you're caught up in chaos, you can simply touch your three fingers and get a burst of serenity and self-esteem.

5. Be outrageous. Throw Nerf balls at the walls, shouting, "I am king of the world!"

6. Gain perspective. Ecclesiastes says, "That which is done is that which shall be done: and there is no new thing under the sun." Or as my mother always said in times of crisis, "Fifty years from now, none of this will matter."

7. Be completely present. Instead of fighting the frenzy, accept yourself as part of it. Be there fully. My mother also liked to quote Ecclesiastes: "Whatsoever thy hand findeth to do, do it with thy might." Enjoy the pressure; it's part of being fully alive. Find the serenity at the center of it all.

8. Take off your shoes and wiggle your toes.

## WHEN YOU'RE WORKING TOO HARD

One proposal writer worked such long hours, he lost track of days and nights. One evening he came home, took off his clothes, took a shower, dried off, put on clean clothes, and was walking out the door before he realized it was dark outside. Was it night or predawn? Was he coming home or going to work?

Working on a big proposal can take over your life. For one big proposal, our team worked for four months. During the last month, we worked twelve-hour days, seven days a week. After the proposal went off on the plane, the proposal manager gave us all three days off. It took me the full three days to recover. I still dreamed about the proposal. I'd wake up in the middle of the night with a start, thinking: *Did I remember to revise the project schedule to reflect that change in Task 17?* Gradually, I'd realize I didn't have to worry about Task 17 anymore. My body was simply tired, but my brain was worthless.

Working too hard on a proposal can also separate you from family members. Valerie, a technical writer, was working on one of those monster proposals that consumes your life. It was big and it was messy, and the engineers kept making last minute changes. On the last day before the proposal was due out, Valerie's fifteen-year-old daughter called to tell her there were bees in the house.

"Well, swat them," said Valerie.

An hour later her daughter called again. "Mom, you've got to come home and help me with these bees."

"Honey, I can't possibly leave right now. Just go upstairs and close your door. Maybe the bees will go to sleep if you do."

About two in the morning, Valerie came home. The house was dark, so she figured her daughter had somehow coped with the bees. As she walked across the darkened living room, she heard the crunch of something under her feet. When she turned on the light, she saw the entire floor was covered in dead bees. "Oh, my poor baby."

Valerie's resourceful daughter, having called a bee expert to divert most of the swarm into a new hive, was safely in bed. But Valerie was shaken.

## ACHIEVING A BALANCE

What can you do to avoid alienating yourself from life? What can you do to make the transition back to life easier? I think the secret is how you enter that proposal cocoon in the first place. You can go into it in a state of terror, frantic to write the proposal. This terror drains energy, leaving you a limp rag at the end.

Instead, let's try to build a cocoon of intense focus without the anxiety—just purposeless tension. Let's try not to waste energy on worrying and shrieking around while we work. But we can't just kick back, either, or we'd never get the proposal done. Zen meditation can bring serenity, a sense of peace, but we need to be careful not to achieve inertial tranquillity. What you want is a serene intensity, a heightened perception of the world. The way you feel when you first fall in love.

I remember capturing that serene but heightened intensity on Kauai. This trip, I had left my laptop at home, taking only a notebook and thinking to write each afternoon. But that pure, moisture-laden air on Kauai led to languor and a quiet, smiling acceptance of measuring the day by the tides and the changing light on the water. Gauging the time by the afternoon wind and the quick rain just after sunset.

One day when we were sitting idly on Tunnels Beach, my sister nudged me and said, "Look at that. It's a Renoir, isn't it?" Two older women were standing with their backs to us in about a foot of water. Both had creamy white skin and were wearing wide-brimmed straw hats and flowered bathing suits in muted tones—the old-fashioned kind of bathing suit that has a little flared skirt to cover the tops of the thighs. Beyond them was the celadon water moving in changing lights over the coral and the endless cloudless sky. In our usual frantic pace back home, we would never have noticed this beauty.

Take time during the proposal pressure to step outside the rush to notice the rest of life. Five minutes here and there won't make or break your proposal's success. Know that you may also be clinging to the proposal because you'll miss the excitement once it's over. Truman Capote said:

Finishing a book is just like you took a child out in the yard and shot it.

Let it go. You *will* recover.

## LEAVING NO TRACE AND GETTING BEYOND

If you can enter the proposal cycle with a purposeless tension, you will find a way to get the job done without becoming a hostage to it. In this book, you've learned to approach the proposal serenely by taking it in easy stages that require no firm commitment. You've learned to

- start by listening to your buyers to discover their needs.
- play with ideas until you find your innovative approach.
- build a temporary structure for your proposal and then draft freely without considering the outcome.
- refine your proposal to make it the best you can.
- let the proposal go on time and on budget.

Once it's over, you can forget the proposal:

> You can start recognizing family members.
> You can do your laundry and eat real meals.
> You can see how much easier it will be next time.

# Relishing Rejection and Savoring Acceptance

●

## 21

*To Enjoy the Flavor of Life,*

*Take Big Bites!*

  —Slogan of the Ultimate Cookie Wholesale Bakery, San Francisco

●

I was persuaded by prudent friends not to call this chapter "The Editor's But," as in "We loved the proposal, but . . ." I'm sure you can recite the reasons along with me:

- But it doesn't fit into our overall program.
- But it's just not quite right for our list.
- But we feel we have to pass.
- But funding will not be available this year.
- But the reviewers felt that your proposal would be successful if it were submitted to a different division.

Olivia Goldsmith had twenty-six rejections for her first novel, *The First Wives Club*. At first, they were postcards and form letters. When she finally got a personally written letter, it said something like "We hate this book, and we never want you to send us anything else, ever again." Her first thought was: *Ah, now I'm a professional writer.*

## REDUCING THE ODDS OF REJECTION

Sending a proposal should be a planned action, based on solid research, not a whim based on synchronicity or astrology or because you happen to know a name. Doesn't hurt, but it wastes postage and your time and the reviewer's time.

Max Yoder, who reviewed proposals for the Chief of Naval Research, says:

> Know your odds! Be a good gambler. Don't "shotgun" your proposal—it's almost always a waste of your time and that of the reviewer. I once received a proposal entitled "An Investigation of the Mobility of the Prairie Chicken on the Nebraska Plain." While it may have been an outstanding proposal, it was inappropriate for the electronics research program I was funding!

## RELISHING REJECTION

Relishing rejection doesn't mean simply wallowing in faint praise. To relish means to savor, to taste fully, to suck the juices out of the bones. And what those juices *are* is a way to learn from each rejection.

Young scientists who submit grant applications to the National Institutes of Health (NIH) know with certainty that they will not win a grant on the first try. When they get the rejection, they don't exactly shoot their fists into the air and shout, "Yes!" But they are grateful because the rejection includes criticism and recommendations for improving the proposal. In fact, submitting proposals to the NIH repeatedly had become so much the natural process that the NIH decided to limit grant writers to three submittals.

John, an editor for a major publishing house, says he feels the word *rejection* is too loaded with negative feelings. He prefers to say he declined a book or passed on it. As if the book is certainly wonderful and someone else will probably make a million on it, but . . .

And there we are, back to the editor's but.

Most writers do learn to relish rejection. Some misguided writers send their rejection letters along with their book proposal to the next editor. Why? Because along with saying they wouldn't publish it, couldn't imagine anyone else publishing it, and pity the poor publisher that takes it on, the letter said that the work was "very solid." Don't ever do this.

Writers watch their mailboxes for the thin envelope. Remember when you were applying to colleges and you hoped for the *thick* envelope that would contain all the forms needed because you'd been accepted? For writers, that thick envelope contains their manuscript, neatly returned and using up all those stamps. But, ah, the *thin* envelope may contain an acceptance. My writer friend Gene remembers coming home each day and closing his eyes before he reached into the mailbox. If his fingers did not touch a big, thick envelope, he opened his eyes.

Writing proposals for the government takes you through three or four levels of anticipation of acceptance or rejection. More and more, government agencies now want a short white paper first. They can review these papers quickly, and if you're rejected at this stage, you can relish rejection because you have saved yourself the time and cost of writing a full proposal. Some agencies even ask for a one-page slide summary *before* the white paper.

So by the time you are writing the proposal, you have made it through at least one hurdle. You now have another chance for rejection. If the proposal is accepted, programs like the Advanced Technology Program then ask you to come for an oral defense of your proposal. You must now present your ideas, then answer questions from ten or twelve people for two or three hours. Being rejected before this stage could be a wondrous relief for people who fear talking in front of a group.

Abhoyjit, a chemical engineer, made it through the white paper, the proposal, and the oral defense. As he left after two hours of questions—feeling it had gone well—they handed him a folder that requested all kinds of financial and contractual information, due within seventy-two hours. If he'd been rejected earlier, he could have avoided all this quite nicely. Instead he survived it all and won $3 million to start a new company.

To truly relish rejection, you need to garner the small positive from the large negative. Think: They actually read it! They didn't throw it on the floor and stomp on it. They didn't stamp it REJECT. Someone at the publishing company or client's office actually touched it.

For the proposal to a business client, you are not as likely to get rejected, because you won't write the proposal to a business executive until after you've sold the company on the idea. You will have met with various people at that company, they will have taken your proposal up the line, and they will have come back to you with demands for revision of the Statement of Work. You have already negotiated the cost. By the time you send them your proposal, you know they are ready to buy.

Sending a proposal to a Japanese company follows much the same routine, except that your formal proposal sets off an avalanche of questions and demands for more information. Consider your formal proposal to the Japanese—no matter how much you've discussed it with them and revised it for them—as a preliminary draft. Your proposal is a starting shot that, after many faxes and e-mails, will culminate in exactly what the Japanese company wants. You are obligated to respond because you have made the first move. Only on pain of a lifetime of shame will you pull your cards off the table.

Relishing rejection letters for your book means turning the negatives into positives.

- Not right for their list? Then whose list is it right for?
- They just published another book like it? Revise your proposal to show how your book is different from what's already out there.
- Too small a market? Find the publisher who is trying to reach that small, but specific, market. And say so in your proposal. An editor for Harper-SanFrancisco says he looks for a book that will sell twenty thousand copies in the first year. If your book can't do that, find a small niche publisher or a university press.

Your book proposal should not tell them how many copies you predict your book will sell. But you can gracefully tell them who you think your readers will be. Let's say you're writing a book about military brats living overseas: the effects on their lives and the effects of their presence on the citizens of Europe and the Far East. Did you know that more than six million American kids went to schools overseas during the Cold War? Bet your publisher didn't, either.

## SAVORING ACCEPTANCE

Now that you've learned to relish rejection, you are free to savor acceptance. Start practicing now. But won't that jinx it? Not at all.

When I bought my first new car, I was so excited I wouldn't let myself believe it. They let me drive it off the lot, saying it would take about three days for the loan to be approved. Absolutely sure they wouldn't approve the loan, I refused to allow myself to believe the car was really mine. I imagined I was just renting it for a few days, then I would return it. When the loan *was* approved, I realized I'd denied myself something important. Instead of glorying in the swift turns and solid brakes of this little car, I had held my feelings back. I'd lost forever the pleasure of the first three days of driving my first brand-new car.

> Die in your thoughts every morning and you will no longer fear death.
>
> —HAGAKURE

If you start savoring acceptance now, even before you've submitted your proposal, you can increase your time for enjoying this pleasure. Even if the proposal is rejected, you have, for a brief time, felt the glory. More important, you've also given yourself the uninterrupted, tranquil, sweet time to savor it fully. When the proposal *is* accepted, the good news will probably come in the middle of other distractions. Here are two stories.

A chemical engineer submitted a proposal to a major chemical company. If he won the proposal, it would mean half a million in research funds and half a million as pure profit. Because the proposal was a national competition and such a long shot, he felt he had little chance of winning. If he didn't win, his job was shaky, so he started looking around. He got an offer for a great new job and had faxed his acceptance when he heard he'd won the million-dollar contract! Now what? Rather than being able to enjoy all the excitement of winning the big contract, he had to wrestle with the decision: Is a fax legal, or can I still back out? Should I stay here with the million dollars or accept the new job? He stayed.

My older sister won a grant to coauthor (with an eighty-year-old artist friend named Dorr) a book on color theory. Here's how she described the awarding of the grant:

When Dorr got the call last Monday from New York, she was out in her garden overseeing two men from the fire department who were cornering a rattlesnake in her ivy. She had started digging there when God (protecting her, as always) sent by her friend Helen, who told her a rattlesnake might be in there. Sure enough, they saw his head and called the fire department.

This is where the call from New York comes in: Helen went to the phone and said Dorr was busy. The vice president of the foundation told her that what he had to say was *far* more important than a rattlesnake. At which point, Dorr was called in to the phone to discover she had won a grant that was three times more than she has ever made a year in her life.

Isn't that the way life is? You can go for years with one dull day after the other and then have the excitement of a rattlesnake in your garden and winning a big grant all on the same day.

## LEARN TO RELISH REJECTION AND SAVOR ACCEPTANCE

Take time to relish rejection because you can

- Learn from it.
- Save time, if you're rejected early in the game.
- Recycle the proposal to another client.

Start enjoying acceptance right now while you have the tranquillity to savor it. Go off someplace where no one will hear you and shout out whatever news you yearn to celebrate:

I won the contract!
I sold my book!
I got the grant!
We launched the spin-off!
We're going public!

# Other Resources

## THE PHILOSOPHY OF ZEN

Boorstein, Sylvia, *It's Easier Than You Think: The Buddhist Way to Happiness* (Harper-SanFrancisco, 1997). "Using powerful stories from everyday experience, Sylvia demystifies spirituality, charts the path to happiness through the Buddha's basic teachings, eliminates hindrances to clear seeing, and finally develops a realistic course toward wisdom and compassion."

———, *Don't Just Do Something, Sit There: A Mindfulness Retreat with Sylvia Boorstein* (HarperSanFrancisco, San Francisco, 1996).

Field, Rick, with Peggy Turner, Rex Weyler, and Rick Ingrasci, *Chop Wood Carry Water: A Guide to Finding Spiritual Fulfillment in Everyday Life* (Jeremy P. Tarcher, Inc., Los Angeles, 1984).

Hanh, Thich Nhat, *Peace Is Every Step: The Path of Mindfulness in Everyday Life* (Bantam Books, New York, 1992). For simple stories with strong meaning, read this or any of his books.

Herrigel, Eugen, *Zen in the Art of Archery* (Pantheon Books, New York, 1953).

Rexroth, Kenneth, *One Hundred Poems from the Japanese* (Norton, 1976). The best and most sensitive translations of Japanese poetry.

Schiller, David, *The Little ZEN Companion* (Workman Publishing, New York, 1994).

St. Ruth, Diana, *Sitting: A Guide to Buddhist Meditation* (Penguin Arkana, New York, 1998).

Suzuki, D. T., *An Introduction to Zen Buddhism* (Grove, 1987). The history and spirit of Zen from the writings of one of the early exponents of Zen in English.

Watts, Alan, *The Way of Zen* (Vintage Books, New York, 1989). A profound yet highly readable introduction to the background and history of Zen as well as its principles and practice.

Winokur, Jon, *Zen to Go* (New American Library, Dutton, 1990). A fine, irreverent collection of Zen attitudes, quoting everyone from Zen Masters to jazz artists and baseball players.

## TOOLS AND GUIDELINES FOR WRITING

Adams, John R., Veda Charrow, and Frank B. Phillippi, *Be a Better Writer: A Manual for EPA Employees* (Environmental Protection Agency, 1980).

Bernstein, Theodore M., *The Careful Writer: A Modern Guide to English Usage* (Atheneum, New York, 1977). The bible for good usage. Arranged in alphabetical order so you can easily find the difference between *which* and *that* or what's wrong with using *hopefully.*

———, *Miss Thistlebottom's Hobgoblins: The Careful Writer's Guide to the Taboos, Bugbears and Out-Moded Rules of English Usage* (Farrar, Straus & Giroux, 1971).

Dodd, Janet S., ed., *The ACS Style Guide: A Manual for Authors and Editors* (American Chemical Society, Washington, D.C., 1997). Designed for chemists, but useful for anyone. Includes chapters on planning and writing the scientific paper; grammar, style, and usage; and making effective oral presentations.

Munter, Mary, *Guide to Managerial Communication: Effective Business Writing and Speaking* (Prentice-Hall, Inc., Englewood Cliffs, N.J., 1999), 5th ed. A very clear step-by-step guide to organizing, drafting, and editing your writing. Also covers how to prepare and deliver presentations.

Schoenfeld, Robert, *The Chemist's English: With "Say it in English, Please!"* (VCH Publishers, Weinheim, Germany, 1990), 3rd ed. "This book is too good to be confined to chemists: the message is there for all scientists." Schoenfeld, an Australian chemist, explains the intricacies of English grammar in a way scientists can understand, including a chapter called "A Chemical Analysis of the English Sentence."

Strunk, Jr., William, and E. B. White, *The Elements of Style* (Macmillan Publishing Company, New York, 1979), 3rd ed. "No book in shorter space, with fewer words, will help any writer more than this persistent little volume." The later editions are available in paperback, but you can always find the hardback first edition of this treasure in used-book stores. It's also on the Internet (www.bartleby.com/index.html). Read it once a year.

## APPROACHES TO WRITING

Dupré, Lyn, *Bugs in Writing: A Guide to Debugging Your Prose* (Addison-Wesley, 1998), 2nd ed. Dupré teaches you to use your "ear" to distinguish bad and ugly writing from good and superb writing.

Goldberg, Natalie, *Writing Down the Bones: Freeing the Writer Within* (Random House, 1998). This classic is widely used in college writing classes. Goldberg is a Zen Buddhist and writing instructor.

———, *Thunder and Lightning: Cracking Open the Writer's Craft* (Bantam, August 2000).

Kilpatrick, James J., *The Writer's Art* (Andrews, McMeel & Parker, Inc., Kansas City/New York, 1985). A beautifully written book that gives examples of the kind of writing that is "awfully wrong, that is less than quite right, that is okay, that is quite beautiful." Includes chapters entitled "The Things We Ought Not to Do" and "The Things We Ought to Be Doing."

Lamott, Anne, *Bird by Bird: Some Instructions on Writing and Life* (Doubleday, 1995). This book is the perfect consolation to a writer and has gathered a large, delighted audience. Writers on the Web say they use her book as a major reference.

Mayfield, Marlys, *Thinking for Yourself: Developing Critical Thinking Skills Through Reading and Writing* (Wadsworth Publishing Company, Belmont, Calif., 2000), 5th ed. Based on the premise that writing is clear when thinking is clear, this college textbook is designed to teach writing through an emphasis on the thinking process and to teach critical thinking through writing.

National Book Award Authors, *The Writing Life: A Collection of Essays and Interviews* (Random House, New York, 1995). Successful writers tell about the perils and pleasures of writing.

Saltzman, Joel, *If You Can Talk You Can Write: A Proven Program to Get You Writing & Keep You Writing* (Warner Books, 1993). An easy-to-read book based on the author's writing course at UCLA.

Stoff, Bill, *Write to the Point: And Feel Better About Your Writing* (Columbia University Press, New York, 1991). With a foreword by Clifford Stoll, who wrote *The Cuckoo's Egg: Tracking a Spy Through the Maze of Computer Espionage.* A good book for people who are insecure about their writing. Stoff shows how to find something to say, to say what you mean to say, and to say it as simply as you can.

Zinsser, William, *Writing to Learn: How to Write—and Think—Clearly About Any Subject at All* (Harper & Row Publishers, New York, 1993). Zinsser wrote this book "to try to ease two fears that American education seems to inflict on all of us in some form. One is the fear of writing. Most people . . . would almost rather die than do it. The other is the fear of subjects we don't think we have an aptitude for." The central point of the book is that we write to find out what we know and what we want to say. He shows how writing even the simplest document can clarify your half-formed ideas.

————, *On Writing Well: An Informal Guide to Writing Nonfiction* (HarperCollins, New York, 1998).

## WRITING BOOK PROPOSALS

Collier, Oscar, and Frances S. Leighton, *How to Write and Sell Your First Nonfiction Book* (St. Martin's Press, 1994).

Cool, Lisa Collier, *How to Write Irresistible Query Letters* (Writer's Digest Books, 1990).

Herman, Jeff, and Deborah M. Adams, *Write the Perfect Book Proposal: 10 Proposals That Sold and Why* (John Wiley & Sons, Inc., 1993).

Larsen, Michael, *How to Write a Book Proposal* (Writer's Digest, 1995), and his chapter, "Sell Your Book Before You Write It," in *The Portable Writers' Conference* (Stephen Blake Mettee, ed., Quill Driver Books/Word Dancer Press, Inc., 1997).

Lyon, Elizabeth, *Nonfiction Book Proposals Anyone Can Write: How to Get a Contract and an Advance before Writing Your Book* (Blue Heron Publishing, Inc., 1995).

## MAKING PRESENTATIONS

Munter, Mary, *Guide to Managerial Communication: Effective Business Writing and Speaking* (Prentice-Hall, Inc., Englewood Cliffs, N.J., 1999), 5th ed. Gives good pointers for preparing presentations as well as advice on writing.

Sarnoff, Dorothy, with Gaylen Moore, *Never Be Nervous Again* (Fawcett, 1997). Dorothy Sarnoff, a well-known speech expert, gives her time-tested method for "foolproof control of nervousness in communicating situations." Easy to read and to learn from.

## CREATIVITY

Bradbury Ray, *Zen in the Art of Writing: Releasing the Creative Genius Within You* (Bantam Books, New York, 1992).

Cameron, Julia, *The Artist's Way: A Spiritual Path to Higher Creativity* (G. P. Putnam's Sons, New York, 1995). This book is a course in discovering and recovering your creative self.

Feynman, Richard P., *Surely You're Joking, Mr. Feynman! Adventures of a Curious Character* (Norton, New York, 1997). Funny stories and outrageous adventures of this creative winner of the Nobel Prize in physics. The introduction describes "his almost compulsive need to solve puzzles, his provocative mischievousness, his indignant impatience with pretension and hypocrisy, and his talent for one-upping anybody who tries to one-up him!"

Goldberg, Natalie, *Wild Mind: Living the Writer's Life* (Bantam, 1990). Advice and exercises for finding your own creative power. One of her rules for learning to trust your own mind is, "You are free to write the worst junk in America."

Kerouac, Jack, *The Dharma Bums* (Penguin Books, New York, 1987). Read it, not so much as a novel, but as a chance to experience the zest of hiking in the Sierras while composing haiku or to listen in on the characters talking Zen philosophy over jugs of red wine in Marin County.

Steinbeck, John, *Journal of a Novel: The* East of Eden *Letters* (Penguin Books, New York, 1990). The day-to-day story of the insights and frustrations of creativity in the form of letters Steinbeck wrote to his friend and editor each day as he was writing *East of*

*Eden.* For example, "I am having such trouble this week—it is a sloppy slippery week. My work does not coagulate. It is as unmanageable as a raw egg on the kitchen floor."

Woolridge, Susan Goldsmith, *Poemcrazy: Freeing Your Life with Words* (Three Rivers Press, New York, 1996). Even if you never, ever plan to write a poem, this book will inspire you to free your thinking (soar!) about how and what you write! Read it just for the love of words.

# Index

## About the Author

As a technical writer in Silicon Valley for twenty-five years, KITTA REEDS has written or edited proposals ranging from a two-page book proposal to a two hundred-page research proposal that brought in $25 million. Formerly a manager of publications for SRI International, a research and innovation company in Silicon Valley, she now conducts workshops on writing winning proposals on both coasts. Kitta lives with her family near San Francisco. Send your proposal-writing experiences to KittaReeds@netscape.net.